Letting Go

OF
WORRY
AND
ANXIETY

PAM VREDEVELT

Multnomah® Publishers *Sisters, Oregon*

LETTING GO OF WORRY AND ANXIETY
published by Multnomah Publishers, Inc.

© 2001 by Pam Vredevelt
International Standard Book Number: 1-57673-955-4

Cover design by The Office of Bill Chiaravalle
Cover image by Artville

Unless otherwise noted, Scripture quotations are from:
The Holy Bible, New International Version © 1973, 1984
by International Bible Society,
used by permission of Zondervan Publishing House

Also quoted:
The Message © 1993 by Eugene H. Peterson
Holy Bible, New Living Translation (NLT) © 1996.
Used by permission of Tyndale House Publishers, Inc. All rights reserved.
New American Standard Bible® (NASB) © 1960, 1977, 1995
by the Lockman Foundation. Used by permission.

Multnomah is a trademark of Multnomah Publishers, Inc.,
and is registered in the U.S. Patent and Trademark Office.
The colophon is a trademark of Multnomah Publishers, Inc.

Printed in the United States of America

For information:
MULTNOMAH PUBLISHERS, INC. • P.O. BOX 1720 • SISTERS, OR 97759

Library of Congress Cataloging-in-Publication Data

Vredevelt, Pam W., 1955–
    Letting go of worry and anxiety / by Pam Vredevelt.
        p. cm.
Includes bibliographical references.
ISBN 1-57673-955-4 (pbk.)
    1. Worry—Religious aspects—Christianity. 2. Anxiety—Religious aspects—
Christianity. 3. Peace of mind—Religious aspects—Christianity. I. Title.
    BV4908.5 .V74 2001
    152.4'6—dc21   2001004686

02 03 04 05 06 07—10 9 8 7 6 5 4 3 2 1

CONTENTS

Acknowledgments

MY THANKS TO BILL JENSEN FOR INVITING ME TO WRITE A series of books that address the emotional struggles we all experience from time to time. Your zeal for releasing fresh perspectives in print is contagious and ignites creativity. It is a marvelous privilege to work under your leadership.

John and I want to thank Don and Brenda Jacobson for your friendship and genuine interest in releasing ministry through us. Your interactions with others, both personally and professionally, display the character of God. We feel honored to be a part of your lighthouse beam.

My heartfelt thanks to Holly Halverson, Judith St. Pierre, and Jennifer Gott for shaping and fine-tuning this manuscript. I lean on your professional expertise, and I'm grateful for your refining touches. Due to your eagle eyes on task, this book is a smooth, easy read.

I also want to say thank you to the Multnomah sales force for catching the vision for this series. Your enthusiasm to get these messages into the marketplace has blessed me and encouraged me to keep writing. John and I cover you in prayer when you are on the front lines. May God grant you unprecedented favor.

Finally, my love to my husband, John, and children, Jessie, Ben, and Nathan, for being the greatest gifts I have ever received.

ARE WORRY AND ANXIETY ROBBING YOU OF PEACE?

The mind by itself can create either
heaven or hell inside of us.

JOHN MILTON

I ONCE HEARD A STORY ABOUT AN ELDERLY WOMAN WHO liked to frequent Las Vegas. During one of her visits, she was standing in front of a slot machine yanking on that one-armed bandit as if her own bony arm were attached to it. Suddenly she hit the jackpot.

Lights flashed, bells clanged, and shiny quarters gushed down the chute. The old lady filled up two buckets to the rim with quarters. But instead of cashing in the coins for currency, she decided to haul the buckets back to her hotel suite. Hunched over from the weight of the mother lode, Vegas Granny got in the elevator to go up to her room.

As usual, the elevator picked up others along the way. At the first stop, two large men stepped in and (all too conveniently, the old lady thought) placed themselves behind her, one on either side. Poor thing. Fear got the best of her, adrenaline kicked in, and her heart started pumping triple-time…*ba-ba-boom, ba-ba-boom, ba-ba-boom.*

Then she heard an unmistakable command: "Hit the floor!" In a panic she fell facedown, convinced that she was about to meet her Maker.

One of the gentlemen bent over and tapped her gently on the shoulder. "Ma'am," he said, "I was talking to my friend. When I said, 'Hit the floor,' I meant, 'Hit the *hotel* floor.'" He pointed ruefully to the buttons on the elevator console.

When the elevator doors opened, that poor, shaken woman couldn't crawl out fast enough. Back in her room, she was just beginning to regain her composure when a knock on the door sent her adrenaline pumping all over again. "Who's there?" she croaked.

Mustering her courage, she finally opened the door a crack for a peek. A deliveryman stood there holding a dozen red roses.

Granny had hit the jackpot again. Wrapped around each lovely rose was a shiny red bow, and inside each bow was a crisp, rolled-up hundred-dollar bill. The enclosed note explained it all:

> I'm so sorry we scared you.
> Sincerely,
> Eddie Murphy[1]

Elevator experiences! We've all had them—those moments when life catches us off guard and we leap to erroneous conclusions. Anxiety overrides logic, our brains short-circuit, and instead of pushing the button on the console, we do a face-plant on the elevator floor. When the unexpected happens and fear kicks in, it robs us of peace by leading us to assume that the worst is right around the corner.

I recently spoke at a large women's conference. One evening at the dinner table I heard comments like:

"I'm in a really good place right now, but I keep wondering when the other shoe is going to drop."

"My kids are having a great year—knock on wood—but I don't know how long that's going to last."

"Things are going well. But I worry about being too happy because I don't want to be disappointed again."

Anxiety had crept in, and it was blocking these women from enjoying the good times afforded them.

Worry is like a rocking chair.
It gives you something to do but
doesn't get you anywhere.
BERNARD MELTZER

I have yet to meet a person who doesn't feel worried or anxious now and then. It's a prevalent problem in today's frantic, fast-paced, information-overloaded society.

Harvard Business Review has reported that stress-related symptoms account for 60 to 90 percent of medical office visits.[2] The media bombard us with ads for products designed to treat such ailments—Tums, Rolaids, Maalox, Excedrin, Tylenol, Advil—and many of us have these products on the shelves in our homes. Pharmaceutical companies spend huge sums of money developing and marketing medications to treat the physical problems resulting from prolonged anxiety. Tagamet, Zantac, Valium, and Xanax are among the most prescribed drugs in America. Some researchers have concluded that anxiety is currently the most damaging disease in America.[3]

In the twenty years I've been a therapist, I think I've treated more people suffering from anxiety than from any other problem. This parallels national statistics. Anxiety is the most common complaint to psychotherapists and the fifth most common complaint received by doctors. One out of four Americans is diagnosed with an anxiety disorder during his or her lifetime. One-third of the general population experienced a panic attack in the last year.[4] In short, if you struggle with worry and anxiety, you are not alone.

A day of worry is more exhausting
than a day of work.

SIR JOHN LUBBOCK

My interest in this *dis-ease* is far more than professional. I have personally wrestled with it on several levels. It can manifest itself as a simple case of the butterflies before I speak at a large conference. In this case the worry is positive—it triggers just enough adrenaline to allow keen concentration and peak performance. But when anxiety takes a stronger hold and leaves me with racing thoughts, overamped nerves, a dry mouth, rapid heartbeat, and "brain freeze," it's anything but positive. It's a real nuisance.

And there have been times when anxiety has been more than just a pesky problem. Following two traumatic incidents in my life, it was more like a noose around my neck that was progressively squeezing the life out of me. My first bout with heightened anxiety occurred after our first baby died in the womb halfway to term. The second followed the traumatic birth of our youngest son, Nathan, who arrived six weeks early with an unexpected diagnosis of Down syndrome and with severe heart complications. During those emotionally charged and difficult times in my life, I needed concrete ways to combat unwelcome worry and anxiety.

In this book, I am passing on to you some of the solid remedies I found. I continue to use these therapeutic interventions myself, and I pass them on to many clients in my counseling office. My goal is to help you find relief from these troubled states of mind. To that end, I'm not offering you a comprehensive medical or academic dissertation on anxiety, but rather some simple, solid tools you can use on a daily basis to decrease your worry and anxiety.[5]

Anxiety is a thin stream of fear

trickling through the mind.

If encouraged, it cuts a channel into

which all other thoughts are drained.

ARTHUR SOMERS ROCHE

Are you worried about your marriage?

Are concerns about your children keeping you up at night?

Are fears about the stock market or debt sapping your energy reserves?

Are you anxious about your health? Are fears about death ever present?

Are you fretting over whether you're going to be rejected by the college you want to attend or the person you'd like to date?

Are you obsessing about whether you'll be able to get a new job or hang on to the job you have?

Is your imagination running wild with "what ifs"?

If so, read on, my friend. Refillable prescriptions follow.

Because we live in a world filled with unpredictable, threatening situations that are often beyond our control, we will never eliminate stress. But these time-tested and clinically proven techniques *can* keep it from robbing us of peace. As we learn how to let go of worry and anxiety, we can greatly increase our peace of mind and ability to enjoy life.

True peace cannot be kept by force.

It can only be achieved by understanding.

ALBERT EINSTEIN

CHAPTER ONE

REVIEW THE FACTS

You gain strength, courage and confidence

by every experience in which you really stop

and look fear in the face.

You are able to say to yourself,

"I've lived through this…

I can take the next thing that comes along."

You must do the thing you think you cannot do.

ELEANOR ROOSEVELT

YEARS AGO I SAW A CLEVER ACROSTIC FOR THE WORD *FEAR:* False Evidence Appearing Real. When we are fearful, we tend to jump to conclusions based on partial truth instead of on complete and accurate evidence. When something goes wrong and we don't have the facts, we can misinterpret the meaning of an event and immediately forecast the worst-case scenario.

I've heard it said that the more intelligent and creative you are, the more likely you are to worry. Why? Because when people are worried about something, their imaginations paint mental pictures of what they dread most. Those with sharp minds see all the angles of a given predicament, and their creativity enables them to vividly envision every possible miserable outcome.

Recently I experienced a rush of anxiety after an innocent mishap. I gave Nathan his nighttime medication and then left the rest of the family at home while I ran a few errands. An hour later I walked in the door toting an armload of groceries. My husband, John, offered to help carry packages in from the garage. Passing me in the hallway, he said, "You don't need to give Nathan his medicine tonight—I already did."

Instantly my brain jumped into 911 mode. *Danger* alarms sounded.

We had a problem. John didn't know that I had already given Nathan his pill, so now Nathan had a double dose of medication in his body. The medicine was something new we were trying for his ADHD (Attention Deficit Hyperactivity Disorder), and I didn't know the drug's toxicity levels or the potential side effects of higher doses. Fear of the unknown revved up my "obsess-o-meter."

One way to reduce worry and anxiety is to get the facts. For me, that meant immediately getting on the phone with a friend who is a doctor and professional educator specializing in this kind of medication. I asked specific questions about how this medicine acted on the brain and what range of dosage was safe for Nathan's body size. From our brief conversation I learned that Nathan could tolerate the double dose and that he would most likely just feel a little groggy for a while. In the words of the expert, "There was no harm done." Those facts brought me peace.

"You will know the truth,
and the truth will set you free."

JOHN 8:32

Naomi, a former client, spoke with me one afternoon about the worries that tormented her. As we reviewed her history, I learned that a teenage neighbor boy had sexually violated her when she was seven years old. When she came to see me, her oldest son was in the first grade, and Naomi was extremely fearful that what had happened to her would also happen to him.

"Bobby keeps getting invitations to spend the night at his friends' homes," Naomi explained. "I can't let him go. I'm so afraid that something bad might happen to him." Naomi knew that her anxiety was blown out of proportion, but she still couldn't shake it. One of my goals was to help her understand her fears.

"Naomi, the avoidance you're using to cope with these situations is actually driving your anxiety," I said. "This is not the kind of fear you can retreat from in the hope that it will just go away. If you want to beat this fear, you're going to have to face it head-on. You see, the fact is: *Avoidance increases anxiety.*"

Naomi spent the next few months of therapy revisiting and processing her childhood trauma. As she connected her current feelings with the facts of her abuse and grieved the injustice, the pain slowly but surely began to lose its power. One of Naomi's assignments in therapy was to make a list of the facts about her past experience. She then compared it with a list of the facts surrounding Bobby's life. Seeing the specific differences in black and white brought her a measure of relief.

But there was more work to do. Naomi decided to give her son some important information. She bought a children's book about personal safety and taught Bobby how to pay attention to the "uh-oh" in his tummy. He learned that it was very important to "Say no!" and to "Go and tell" an adult if he felt at risk. She rehearsed potential scenarios with Bobby and showed him how to respond to someone who was acting in a sexually inappropriate way. Giving Bobby the facts reduced Naomi's concerns about his vulnerability and increased her confidence in his ability to protect himself.

21

Gathering facts about Bobby's friends and their parents was also helpful. Naomi felt more comfortable with some individuals than with others. She reached a great milestone when she and her husband gave Bobby permission to spend the night with his best friend after a ball game. It didn't happen without some anxiety, but it happened!

To keep herself from worrying, Naomi used a diversion tactic that evening: She and her husband went to see an action-packed movie. During our next counseling session, she happily reported that she had slept well through the night. As for Bobby, when he came home in the morning, he was beaming.

The adventurous life is not one exempt from fear, but on the contrary, one that is lived in full knowledge of fears of all kinds, one in which we go forward in spite of our fears.

PAUL TOURNIER

Are worries stealing your joy? Are anxieties eating away at your peace of mind? If so, may I make a suggestion? Please—

get the facts. If you're fretting about the possibility of a health problem, don't brood over it. Call a doctor or see a specialist who can review the facts with you. Focus your attention on *what is,* not on *what if.* Investigate. Ask questions. Research. Pool information. A mind that feeds on the facts is less likely to fall prey to a frenzied imagination that casts illusions as reality. The fear of the unknown can paralyze you, but reviewing the facts can set you free and give you peace.

22

Peace is not arbitrary.
It must be based upon definite facts.
God has all the facts on His side;
the world does not.
Therefore God, and not the world,
can give peace.

BILLY GRAHAM

CHAPTER TWO

REGISTER YOUR CONCERNS WITH GOD

Don't fret or worry. Instead of worrying, pray.

Let petitions and praises shape your worries into prayers,

letting God know your concerns.

Before you know it, a sense of God's wholeness,

everything coming together for good,

will come and settle you down.

PHILIPPIANS 4:6–7, *THE MESSAGE*

MY SECRETARY STOOD IN THE DOORWAY OF MY OFFICE, her face registering her alarm.

"Pam, you have an emergency phone call," she said. "Nathan left the schoolyard. They've searched for the last half hour and can't find him, so they're calling the police."

That news would send icy shivers through any mother, but my fear escalated in light of my son's Down syndrome. Nathan lacks the safety net of common sense and maturity, and when he wanders outside of adult supervision, his risk of encountering danger increases exponentially.

Adrenaline coursing through my veins, I rushed to the phone my secretary held for me. "Hello, this is Pam," I said, trying to maintain my cool. "I'm on my way."

It's astounding what anxiety does to the body. By the time I reached my car, my stomach was in knots, and a lump the size of a Ping-Pong ball seemed wedged against my larynx. I began playing therapist with myself.

Okay, Pam. Calm down. God knows right where Nathan is.

There are a lot of people looking for him. Keep your cool. Don't jump to conclusions. You won't be any help to anybody if you start short-circuiting. Just relax. You'll be at the school in five minutes.

That was the plan. But you know how plans go.

When I started the car, a buzzer signaled that my gas tank was empty. I had intended to get gas on the way to work that morning, but I was running late. I figured I could make it to the office and fill the tank after work.

Now, what do you think a professional therapist would do in a situation like this? Would she respond with logic and say, "Hmm. It looks like I need gas"? Would she maintain complete composure, casually shrug, and say, "Oh well, what's another kink in the day"? Or would she flail her hands, scream "Oh no!" at the gas gauge, and then burst into tears?

You guessed it! Obviously my car wasn't the only thing running on fumes at the moment. After my little fit, I pulled myself together long enough to pray, *God, please get me to the gas station that's on the way to the school.*

He did. But I should have prayed for the people at the station because they were slower than slugs on a Portland sidewalk. For several l-o-o-o-n-g minutes, my car was the only one at the pumps, but no one responded. If the Lord was testing my patience, I flunked. After waiting and waiting, I finally went into the station and said, "Could someone please help me? I'm in a hurry. My little boy is lost, and I need to go find him."

The guy dawdling behind the counter acted as if he didn't have a care in the world. He cocked his head to the side, squinted his eyes, and gave me the look. You know—the one that says, "Yeah, sure, lady." He s-l-o-o-o-w-l-y made his way to the pumps.

Twelve and one-half minutes later, I rolled out of the station with enough repressed negative energy in my body to trigger another eruption on Mount Saint Helens.

26

Anxiety is the interest paid

on trouble before it is due.

DEAN WILLIAM R. INGE

Panic-driven thoughts ricocheted in my brain. *What if we can't find Nathan? What if he wanders onto a busy street? What if a felon gets hold of him?* Pictures on milk cartons flashed before my eyes. A vivid imagination is a blessing for creative writing, but it's a curse in these kinds of situations.

I finally arrived at the school. Racing up to the front doors, I passed a woman walking toward the parking lot. I must have had *panicked mother* written all over my face, because she looked at me and asked, "Are you Nathan's mom?"

"Yes," I responded anxiously, hoping she had some good news for me.

"They found Nathan."

"Oh, thank God," I said.

"He's with the principal," she added.

Sure enough. There in the principal's office sat my guilty little escapee. I couldn't remember an occasion when Nathan hadn't smiled and jumped up to give me a welcoming hug after we'd been apart for a few hours. But this time he had a very somber look on his face, and he didn't move. His head hung low, and he looked at me through guilty eyes, knowing he had made a *big* boo-boo.

I hugged him. "Nathan," I said gently, "I was very worried about you. And the principal and your teachers were scared, too. Leaving the schoolyard was not a good idea."

The principal gave me the full story. Somehow Nathan had sneaked around to the back of the school, pushed the gate open, and wandered over to the retirement home next door. He went to the third floor of the complex (Nathan loves elevators and is proficient at working them), roamed the halls, and then went back down to the ground level and out the back door. I guess he'd seen enough of the old folks and decided it was time for something a bit more exciting.

Driven by his unquenchable thirst for adventure, he bolted over to the next building on the block, which happened to be a hospital. There a kind elderly man noticed that Nathan was handicapped and all alone in the hospital lobby. Figuring that he was lost, the man took him by the hand and began hunting. A few minutes later, one of the school helpers in the search party rounded the corner.

Nathan spent the rest of the afternoon in the principal's office with the school counselor. She drew pictures of the event to help him understand which choices were acceptable and which were not. I am so thankful for such sources of support as we try to help Nathan grow up to be safe and wise. Still, I think I pumped more adrenaline during that episode than I had the entire previous month.

And, boy oh boy, did my body feel it the next day! When the alarm went off at 5:30 A.M., I felt as if I'd been hit by a Mack truck. The impact wasn't just physical. My mind was troubled, and worry was getting the best of me. My anxiety about the events of the previous day was matched by my apprehension of what was to come.[1]

A worried man could borrow a lot of trouble with practically no collateral.

HELEN NIELSEN

Do you ever experience that? Ever have a day so full of panic that, even after a situation is resolved, the residue of fear taints your outlook? At times like that, we need to take some time alone to register our concerns with God. He invites us to do so. The apostle Peter wrote: "Cast all your anxiety on him because he cares for you" (1 Peter 5:7). In the original language this phrase means that we are "to aggressively roll over" all of our worries onto God.

Let's think for a moment about how we are created. We are made up of body, soul, and spirit. Through our body's senses, we relate to the world around us. Our soul is the thinking and feeling part of us: our mind, will, emotions, conscience, and consciousness. Our soul allows us to laugh, cry, reason, and make choices. Then there is our spirit, which enables us to relate to God.

I have noticed that human beings tend to use only two-thirds of this package. Even if we try to use the capacities of our body and soul to the fullest, we may neglect our spirit. Yet God longs to have a personal relationship with us and to be intimately involved in the things that matter most to us. One of the reasons He invites us to cast our anxieties on Him is that He is far more capable of bearing those burdens than we are. He never intended for us to carry the stresses, strains, and harsh realities of this world on our own shoulders. He wants us to roll them onto Him and to ask Him for what we need.

29

God is greater than our worried hearts
and knows more about us than we do ourselves.

1 JOHN 3:20, *THE MESSAGE*

One of the ways we can register our concerns with God is by writing them in a prayer journal. Some call it a "worry registry." This is a powerful tool for reducing anxiety, and a number of my clients have benefited from this discipline for years. They buy a new blank book at the beginning of each year and, on a regular basis, record their worries in letters to God.

This kind of journaling serves several purposes. Registering our concerns and needs with God in detail is a very constructive way to defuse the pent-up tension surrounding our worries. Even more importantly, it opens the door for Him to intervene in our lives. We get far better results with His power at work than we do if we depend only on our own limited human resources. Watching concrete, specific answers to prayer unfold over time is a faith-building, life-changing experience. The more people see God answer their prayers, the more they tend to register their concerns.

The morning following Nathan's escape, I made myself a cup of coffee, found a comfortable seat in the living room, jotted down some of my worries, and offered a simple prayer. Nothing complicated—just a soul's cry for help:

Lord, You know how troubled I am about Nathan. I need You to speak to me today. Please give me Your perspective, and help me hear what You want to say to me this morning.

As I read from my Bible, I wrote down some verses that spoke to me about what had taken center stage in my mind:

I will make springs in the desert, so that my chosen people can be refreshed.

ISAIAH 43:20, NLT

I will give you abundant water to quench your thirst and to moisten your parched fields. And I will pour out my Spirit and my blessings on your children. They will thrive like watered grass, like willows on a riverbank.

ISAIAH 44:3–4, NLT

And I will give you treasures hidden in the darkness—secret riches. I will do this so you may know that I am the LORD…the one who calls you by name.

ISAIAH 45:3, NLT

By [God's] mighty power at work within us, he
is able to accomplish infinitely more than we
would ever dare to ask or hope.

EPHESIANS 3:20, NLT

The sequence and content of the verses rang with
meaning. I recorded in my journal what the Lord seemed to be
saying to me:

*Pam, when life escorts you into a hot, dry, barren
desert, look to Me. I always have what you need. I
will refresh you. You can never tap the limit of My
abundant supply. I have enough for you and your
children. I will pour out My Spirit and bless your
children today. They will thrive. And in the middle
of the hardships and the dark times you endure, I
will give you treasures—treasures that can be
found only in the dark—that prove that I love you
and that I am intimately aware of everything going
on in your life. I understand your weaknesses and
vulnerabilities. Don't be fooled by your feelings. My
Spirit lives in you, and He is able to accomplish
more than you have ever imagined. So rest. Trust.
Let My words empower you. They are spirit and
they are your very life.*

I closed my journal that morning with a much healthier
outlook on the day. My body still felt bulldozed, but my mind

was more settled. Even though nothing had really changed on the outside, I was different on the inside. Order and focus had emerged out of a chaotic mishmash of worry and anxiety. Registering my concerns with God had brought me relief.[2]

Are fears wearing you out? Are you carrying heavy weights of worry that you need to unload? Have you considered placing those burdens in the hands of God? He would like nothing more than to intervene on your behalf. Rest assured: God will hear and He will answer. I haven't met a person yet who has regretted turning to God for help. Peace comes when we lift our cares to Him and let them go.

"Call to Me and I will answer you,
and I will tell you great and mighty things,
which you do not know."

JEREMIAH 33:3, NASB

CHAPTER THREE

REQUIRE A PLAN

Four steps to achievement:

Plan purposefully, prepare prayerfully,

proceed positively, pursue persistently.

WILLIAM ARTHUR WARD

WORRY AND ANXIETY TEND TO JUMP-START THE IMAGINATION into overdrive.

Surprisingly, this typically occurs when the mind is quiet. You can disregard something bothering you through the course of a busy day, but once you settle down in the evening for some peace and quiet, those worrisome thoughts start intruding again. After a mostly worry free, fully scheduled day and evening, you can fall into bed exhausted and go to sleep immediately, only to have the anxieties show up in your dreams. Why? Because worry tends to feed on a passive mind.

One of the best remedies for worry is to develop a plan of action *before* your imagination has an opportunity to be reactivated. Developing an advance plan can hold anxiety at bay. Just knowing that you're taking concrete steps to work on a problem can bring relief.

When Nathan was about four years old, we became aware of his marvelous (but hair-raising) sense of adventure. Every so often he threw us a curveball by leaving the house without telling us where he was going. We learned from other parents that this is a common occurrence among children with

Down syndrome. When these youngsters wander, they are simply following through with a fun idea that has come to mind. Because of their limited cognitive abilities, they don't sense the potential danger. Nathan had no idea that his escapes threw all of us into panic mode. He was just having a grand time exploring the world.

For our own peace of mind, we devised a plan. We secured extra bolts to the tops of all doors leading outside. We activated a beeper on our alarm system so we would know whenever a door was opened. We bought Nathan a new identification bracelet and necklace with his name, address, and phone number on them. Each family member agreed to keep a more watchful eye on him, and I even checked into using a local dog-search service in case an emergency occurred and the police weren't able to help. Finally, we consulted a developmental behavioral pediatrician for family counseling. We wanted to find ways to deal with the anxieties Nathan's escapes aroused in all of us.

Each piece of our plan helped increase our sense of control and decrease what we perceived as Nathan's vulnerability to danger.

Many of our fears are tissue-paper thin,

and a single courageous step

would carry us clear through them.

BRENDAN FRANCIS

The specialist we consulted gave us added insight. "The more children are hovered over, the more they'll bolt," he told us. "They'll react against boundaries that are too restricting." Because of his past escapades, we were afraid that Nathan would run off again, and we admitted that he probably sensed us hovering. The doctor suggested that we intentionally ease the restrictions and send him on small, safe, independent missions.

So we developed another plan. Instead of getting the mail ourselves, we asked Nathan to do it for us as we watched (out of Nathan's view) from a window. When he accomplished the task without bolting, we high-fived each other for a job well done. We also started asking him to let the dogs in and out and to help feed them their evening meal.

What the doctor said made sense. Our fear was constricting Nathan, and he was reacting against it. The more freedom we provided for him, the less he needed to push the limits. Developing a plan with the help of an expert made all the difference in the world. I've seen this work for others, too.

All of us can take steps—no matter how small

and insignificant at the start—

in the direction we want to go.

MARSHA SINETAR

I remember counseling Mark, a graduate student who suffered from severe anxiety before major exams. There was an interesting twist to this case: Mark's anxiety was not related to his test performance. This young man was an extremely intelligent, top-notch student who had a photographic memory. The college he attended was highly competitive, and his personal goal was to graduate at the top of his class. The cause of his anxiety was not the fear that he would do poorly on his exams—he was riddled with worry about not waking up in time to get to them.

In his first term at school, he stayed up all night before tests to eliminate the possibility of missing them. That routine was killing him. I suggested that he develop a more realistic plan to reduce his anxiety.

A plan unfolded during the counseling session. Mark decided to set his wristwatch alarm to beep two hours before an exam. This gave him time to wake up, shower, and review his notes before the test. He also set the alarm on his clock radio to blare music full volume from the other side of the room so he had to get out of bed to turn it off. As an added precaution, he asked his roommate to rouse him just in case he slept through both alarms. Last but not least, he enlisted his best friend on campus to knock on his door an hour before the exam to make sure he was up and ready to go.

As you can imagine, the wristwatch alarm was enough to jolt him out of his slumber, and he was on his feet in seconds. Anyone who is that conscientious about his studies isn't going to ignore an alarm. But before he went to bed at night his *imagination* wouldn't let him believe that one alarm was sufficient. To quiet it, he had to develop what he considered to be a fail-safe plan. By the end of his second year of school, Mark's preexam anxieties were under control. The last I heard, he is practicing with a prestigious law firm downtown and sleeping like a baby at night.

Formulating a plan doesn't have to take a lot of time or be a complicated process. It can be as simple as identifying a few specific steps you can take to increase your sense of control.

If you're worried about how you're going to pay your children's college tuition, consult a financial advisor to devise a plan. Investigate the options with someone who can guide you in the process.

If you're worried about your child's academic performance, make a phone call. Connect with the counselors and teachers in the school system. Utilize their input and experience to form and implement a plan. The more support people you can include in the process, the more likely the plan will succeed.

If you're confused or don't know where to go for help in the planning process, ask God. He knows all the ins and outs of the situations that concern you, and He will give you wisdom. Nothing you are facing catches Him by surprise. He is able to lead, guide, and enlighten you about the next step to take. Ultimately, He is the One with all the answers. With your highest welfare in mind, He can help you develop a plan and then give you the power to achieve it.

Commit to the Lord whatever you do,

and your plans will succeed.

PROVERBS 16:3

CHAPTER FOUR

RECONNECT WITH THE PRESENT

Anxiety is not only a pain
which we must ask God to assuage
but also a weakness we must ask Him to pardon—
for He's told us to take no care for the morrow.

C. S. LEWIS

MANY OF OUR WORRIES COME FROM A TENDENCY TO overestimate the probability of a harmful event and to exaggerate its potential negative impact. Peering into the future, our imaginations run wild, leading us to conclude that things are going to turn out badly and with unbearable results.

One of the best ways to stop this needless waste of mental and emotional energy is to live in the moment. Not tomorrow. Not next week. Not next month. But today, right now. I know—it's easier said than done. The human mind likes to wander from the present, particularly when our thought processes aren't focused on something stimulating.

Just last night, I found myself struggling to keep my thoughts in the moment. John and I have a friend who comes to our home every once in a while to give us a massage. There I was, on the massage table, enjoying the warmth of a crackling fire, the melodies of soothing classical music, and the touch of gifted hands, when I suddenly felt a knot in my stomach. I soon realized that my mind was chewing on some problems that needed to be solved before our family traveled out of the country the following week.

While I rehearsed the logistics of the trip, the "what ifs" led me down rabbit trails into anxiety. I imagined us getting bumped from a flight and spending the night in an airport with our three kids. That's not my idea of fun!

A mind that travels to the future or the past is fertile ground for worry and anxiety.

Stop it, I told myself. *You can deal with the details of the trip later. Now is not the time.* To bring myself back to the moment, I refocused on the fire, the music, and the sensations my body was feeling from the massage. A few minutes later, when my stomach knotted up once more, I realized that I was off in the future again. I had to bring myself back to focusing on the here and now three times before my mind finally let go of the impending trip. As long as I stayed in the moment, my body was peaceful and worry free. When I was in the future, my stomach told the story.

By the way, our bodies never lie. They send clear cues to us about what is going on in our minds. We do ourselves a favor when we listen to what our bodies are saying.

Focusing our attention on the moment requires mental discipline, but the contentment it brings is worth it. I can hear you saying, "Now, wait a minute. Isn't it a bit ridiculous to expect myself not to think about the future? How else can I plan for what lies ahead?"

I'm not saying that we should never think about the

future. That's silly. A well-ordered life requires us to plan. Thinking ahead makes sense when it's related to necessary planning, but it can become a problem when most of our thoughts have little connection with the here and now. What I am saying is that we need to try to live in the present *more* than we live in the future. When our minds perpetually spin forward into the future, we generate anxiety and miss the joy of the immediate.

42

Anxiety does not empty tomorrow of its sorrows but only empties today of its strength.

CHARLES SPURGEON

You see, our thoughts powerfully influence our feelings. In a matter of seconds, they can destroy our peaceful state of mind and create panicked anxiety, without anything else changing around us.

A few nights ago, after my husband and I tucked our two youngest children into bed, I hopped in bed myself, nestled under the covers, and opened a good book. There I was, snuggled beneath my warm electric blanket and lost in a story, when the thought occurred: *It's 10:30, and Jessie isn't home yet.* Our teenage daughter had a 10:30 curfew, but she hadn't yet walked through the front door. I brushed it off, figuring that the traffic was bad.

I went back to my book. Ten minutes later, Jessie still wasn't home. This time I didn't brush it off as well. My mind wandered: *It's not like her not to be home on time. I wonder what's going on. I hope she's okay. Why didn't she call to tell me she'd be late?*

Countering the anxious thoughts, I told myself that there was probably a good reason why she was late. But my worry intensified when my creative imagination conjured up a troublesome scene: her friend's car broken down and the kids stuck on the side of the road with no one to help. I overestimated the likelihood that she was in trouble and the probability that the results were going to be harmful.

By the time Jessie arrived thirty minutes later, my mind was anything but calm and serene. She wasn't home on time, and I didn't like it. Coming back to the present allowed me to maintain my cool. I told myself: *She's home. She's safe. Now listen to her*. Had I persisted in my anxious imaginations, my agitation would have reached a boiling point and erupted all over her. Fortunately I was able to contain myself and not blow a fuse before I heard her explanation. My fears, as you might expect, were completely unfounded.

All of the pent-up emotion in my body was simply a by-product of my unchecked, future-oriented thoughts. Once I reviewed the facts and directed my attention back to the present, peace returned. If I had simply kept my mental energies in the here and now, enjoyed my warm blanket and book, and reminded myself of my daughter's resourcefulness and common sense, I would have saved myself a lot of unnecessary grief.

When we forecast gloom and doom into our future, or go back into the past and rake up all the troubles we've had, we end up reeling and staggering through life. Stability and peace of mind come by living in the moment.

Where are your thoughts focused? Are you engaged in

what you're currently doing, or is your imagination running wild in the future, overestimating the likelihood of potential danger? Most of our worries are imaginary. What you think are huge storm clouds in the sky may be nothing more than dust on your eyelashes. So why not blink a few times, shake off the dust, and refocus your sights on the present?

44

"Give your entire attention to what

God is doing right now,

and don't get worked up about what

may or may not happen tomorrow.

God will help you deal with whatever

hard things come up when the time comes."

MATTHEW 6:34, *THE MESSAGE*

CHAPTER FIVE

REACH

OUT

The deepest need of man is the need

to overcome his separateness,

to leave the prison of his aloneness.

ERICH FROMM

WE LIVE IN AN UNPREDICTABLE WORLD THAT EVOKES FEAR, and there isn't a person alive who isn't vulnerable to worry and anxiety. But acknowledging that takes courage. We don't easily admit to feelings of weakness and vulnerability. For the most part, we harbor a subtle contempt for the debilities or deficiencies we perceive in ourselves and others.

As a result, we end up rejecting key parts of our humanity. We gloss over our needs instead of admitting them. We deny, minimize, or at least sidestep many forms of suffering, and we become very creative in the ways we medicate our worries. In the end, we are left to struggle with our anxieties alone in the dark.

This is not God's plan. From the very beginning of time, He has wanted people to enjoy intimate relationship with Him and others. He longs to walk arm-in-arm with us—and to provide empathetic friends to walk with us—through the sorrows and sufferings that are an inevitable part of life in this world.

Connections matter. When we withdraw, detach, or close God and others out of our suffering, we cut off our source of life and derail our own healing. The bottom line is that God never intended for us to try to handle our worries and anxieties alone. Peace comes in the context of relationships.

God knows our propensity to worry and feel anxious, and He wants us to experience His comfort in the midst of our troubles. One of His names is "The God of All Comfort." The word *comfort,* which is mentioned fifty-nine times in the New Testament, literally means "to call near." It evokes a picture of one person calling out to another to come stand alongside him or her. Comfort comes as we risk reaching out, transparent in our pain, and allow others to come near and strengthen us in our troubled state.

I recall a final counseling session with a woman I treated for an anxiety disorder after she had a radical mastectomy. After several months of therapy, during which she grieved her losses, established new goals, and tried a variety of medications before finding the right fit, she was ready to put closure on counseling. I'll never forget her final remark. With tears in her eyes, she grasped my hands tightly and said, "Thank you for befriending my pain."

It had indeed been my privilege. Witnessing her progress spoke volumes to me about the healing power of connecting with safe people to whom we can disclose our deepest conflicts.

As a professional therapist, I spend a lot of time with people in their pain. They need someone to help them sort through their confusion, respond to their suffering, help them get unstuck when they become arrested by grief, and strengthen their will to live when they have been diminished by the cruelties of life. They need someone to validate their afflictions and create a safe place for them to process their pain and let it go. Whether or not a specific problem is solved during a counseling session is sometimes irrelevant. Many issues are not resolved quickly. But healing often happens when a person shares his or her suffering with someone safe.

A safe relationship multiplies our joy
and divides our grief.

I recall an occasion, years ago, when I was overcome with worry. Despite using all the anxiety-reduction tricks I knew, I was unable to shake the fear. It all started with a letter.

After our first baby died in the womb, I wrote *Empty Arms: Emotional Support for Those Who Have Suffered Miscarriage, Stillbirth, or Tubal Pregnancy* to encourage others who were suffering similar losses. Cards and letters poured in from women across the country, thanking me for the book and telling me their own stories of loss.

Four weeks prior to delivering our second baby, I received a letter from a woman who found out during her eight-month exam that her baby had died. The doctor had been unable to detect a heartbeat. The details of her story were nearly identical to our experience with our first baby. As I read her letter, all of the memories of our loss came flooding back like a tidal wave.

I tried everything I knew to quiet my fears. I prayed. I sang. I used thought-stopping methods. I scrubbed the kitchen floor. I tried reading my Bible and some other good books. But the anxiety continued. My imagination was toxic with worry.

Not wanting to burden my husband or evoke any unnecessary fear in him, I carried the anxiety alone. That, by the way, was not a smart move. If there is one thing I learned from that incident, it was this: *Never worry alone!*

The next day at our Sunday morning church service, I asked to talk with our pastor's wife. Even though she and her husband were new to our congregation and I didn't know her well, I felt I could trust her.

"I am riddled with worry," I told her. "I received this letter…and I'm afraid the same thing is going to happen all over again." I knew that the anxiety was irrational. There was no evidence that the baby I carried was in danger. But I also realized that I was powerless to find relief on my own.

Diane listened attentively, and I could tell from her responses that she empathized with my struggle. We joined hands, and she prayed for me and for the baby. Although that connection took only five brief minutes, it brought great relief. Peace went home with me that day. Healing happened as we connected with God and with each other.

When I think back over the times in my life when I was overwhelmed by worry and anxiety, I realize that the greatest moments of relief came when I sensed that God and a trusted friend were truly present with me in my struggle. It was as if they opened the door, walked into my turmoil, sat down with me, and, with full acceptance, waited. My brokenness was our meeting place. Inner peace and healing were born within that connection. Their companionship in my suffering brought relief, even though the circumstances that brought about the distress remained the same.

I have learned that whatever we deny, repress, or hide in the dark cannot be healed but that sharing our concerns openly and exposing them to the light can lead to growth and peace. When your worries seem overwhelming, please resist the temptation to isolate yourself, withdraw, and shrink back in the shadows.

Consider carefully those to whom you can turn for support. Will they listen well? Do they have experience with whatever is troubling you? Do you know that they have your very best interests at heart? Do they have a track record of integrity? Are they healthy enough to offer suggestions and then give you the freedom to make your own decisions?

If so, reach out. It usually takes more than one pair of hands to peel your death grip off your worries so you can let them go.

[Jesus said,] "When two of you get together
on anything at all on earth and make a prayer of it,
my Father in heaven goes into action.
And when two or three of you are
together because of me,
you can be sure that I'll be there."

MATTHEW 18:19–20, *THE MESSAGE*

CHAPTER SIX

RESPECT YOUR NEED FOR RENEWAL

Renewal and restoration are not luxuries.
They are essentials. There is absolutely nothing
enviable or spiritual about a coronary or a
nervous breakdown, nor is an ultrabusy schedule
necessarily the mark of a productive life.

CHARLES SWINDOLL

YEARS AGO, I ATTENDED A PROFESSIONAL SEMINAR WITH A Harvard-trained psychologist who specialized in treating people suffering from anxiety and depression. He made a statement that left a lasting impression on me: "Many patients can reduce their anxiety and depression symptoms by half if they'll sleep eight to nine hours a night." That made sense to me. It's impossible to have sound mental health if we deprive our bodies and ignore our basic physical needs.

It's a common dilemma. We work, raise families, build marriages, tend to friendships, and try to cram in recreational activities. Our daily planners are chock-full of to-do lists, and there are never enough hours in a day to get it all done. Although this is true, we need to remember that sleep is one of the primary ways the body renews itself. If we rob ourselves of sleep by burning the candle at both ends, we impair our ability to let go of the worry and anxiety generated by the unending demands made upon us.

The less you sleep, the more you'll worry.

Cutting our sleep short can negatively impact the quality of our health. It is common knowledge that people who try to live on less than four or five hours of sleep for an ongoing period of time are at higher risk for early death. On the other hand, medical experts agree that consistent, sound sleep reduces anxiety and increases our ability to manage life stress.

I found I could add nearly two hours
to my working day by going
to bed for an hour after lunch.
SIR WINSTON CHURCHILL

During World War II, our prisoners of war suffered extreme sleep deprivation. Whenever they fell asleep, their captors immediately awakened them. After days of this torture, the men became anxious, irritable, confused, and impulsive. During sleep the brain processes are restored, especially the higher-level functions involving concentration and motivation. Deprived of sleep, the prisoners of war revealed military information they typically would have concealed.

Insomnia, or the inability to fall asleep or stay asleep, can be caused by a number of things. Physicians list several common causes: arthritis or other types of chronic pain, endocrine disturbances, the overuse of certain chemical substances such as caffeine and decongestants, withdrawal from alcohol or pain medication, or disturbances in our biological clock that result from traveling across time zones or feeding newborn babies during the wee hours of the morning.

But chemical changes in the brain correlated with depression and anxiety can also cause insomnia. When this is the cause, a vicious cycle can set in. Worry and anxiety can cause insomnia, and insomnia can cause worry and anxiety. This cycle has to be broken for the brain chemistry to restore itself.

None of our babies slept through the night at an early age, so in the months after they were born my routine included many midnight feedings. The babies' needs and my shifting hormones meant months of interrupted sleep. When my body didn't renew itself well during the night, my motivation and energy levels were low the following day. I found myself more easily agitated, anxious, and overalert. There were times when I startled awake in the middle of the night, even though everyone else in the house was sound asleep and there were no external noises. It was as if my body was sending signals that put me into a 911 mode when there were no logical reasons for alarm.

For my own sanity, I knew I needed to do something to stop the sleep deprivation, but I felt stuck. The babies needed to eat, and I was their source. John and I considered a number of options and then formed a plan. He offered to supplement my nursing by giving the babies one bottle-feeding a night so I could get four to five hours of solid sleep. To recharge my batteries for the rest of the day, I also made a point of napping for at least thirty minutes during the day while the babies slept. The household chores had to take a backseat to my health.

After this new routine was established, I noticed a marked difference. My overall mood improved, and I had more energy during the day. Decision-making was easier. Chores weren't as taxing. Little annoyances didn't seem like such a big deal. A few weeks later the random startle responses I was experiencing in the middle of the night subsided.

55

Sleep recreates...sleep is not meant only
for the recuperation of a man's body...
there is a tremendous furtherance of
spiritual and moral life during sleep.

OSWALD CHAMBERS

I recently learned that 40 percent of women over the age of forty experience periodic insomnia. Research scientists speculate that this correlates with the shifting hormone levels that occur prior to menopause. Incidentally, women are more likely to suffer from insomnia than men. Dieting, which women tend to do more often than men, can lower body temperature and interfere with sound sleep.

When we are going through stressful life transitions, our bodies may need even more sleep than usual. I remember talking with a mother whose eleven-month-old son had died after complications from a surgery. "All I want to do is sleep," she said. One of the red flags of depression is the desire to sleep more than necessary, but I sensed that something else was at work here.

After her baby died, this woman had begun a new, full-time job, and she was averaging ten-hour days as an executive assistant. When I asked her how much she slept, she said, "From nine at night to seven in the morning," as if this were a ridiculous amount of time to be in bed. It never crossed her mind that her body needed more sleep because of the heavy emotional burden she was bearing after losing her son and starting a new job. From my perspective, those ten hours of sleep didn't point to pathology; they indicated good self-care.[1]

A heart at peace gives life to the body.

PROVERBS 14:30

All of us have probably found ourselves in problem situations that don't faze us when we are well rested, but level us when we are sleep deprived. The body needs time to renew and replenish itself when we are carrying heavy emotional loads.

Recently I was worried about one of our children. It was the end of a long day, and I was very tired and needed rest. As I crawled into bed, I told myself that fatigue was probably exaggerating my concerns. I knew that I needed to shelve the issue until morning, when I would have enough energy to think straight.

The alarm sounded at 5:45, and I slipped out of bed for

some time alone with God. I read a passage from the Bible, reflected on it, and spoke to God about my concerns. After eight hours of sleep, I was able to review the situation that had troubled me the night before with more mental strength and clarity. New perspectives emerged. Insights came. Nothing had changed regarding the situation evoking the worry, but inside I was calmer and more capable of working on the problem simply because I had gotten some sleep. Our ability to keep anxiety in check often has much to do with how well we are taking care of ourselves.

As you retire to rest, give your soul

and God a time together,

and commit your life to God with

a conscious peace for the hours of sleep,

and deep and profound developments

will go on in spirit, soul, and body

by the kind creating hand of our God.

OSWALD CHAMBERS

Many people have difficulty sleeping because they don't get enough physical activity. In previous generations, people naturally defused daily tensions as they plowed fields, baled hay, and walked to their destinations. By the end of the workday, both the mind and the body were ready for sleep. Nowadays, however, most people are much more sedentary, both on and off the job, and this has made insomnia much more common.

If you find yourself irritable, agitated, anxious, or unable to turn off the lights in your brain at night, physical exercise is prescriptive, not optional. Although I'm not an expert in physiology, as a clinical counselor I know the mental and emotional benefits of exercise. Studies have shown that it is a critical key to managing worry and anxiety. It's a cheap, easy way to elevate mood, decrease agitation, and deliver a sense of calm to the brain. The endorphins released during aerobic exercise, for example, are powerful mood elevators and natural tranquilizers. Because it literally forces tension out of our bodies, exercise is a superb tool for managing the worries that keep us keyed up.

The most frequent rebuttal I hear to the argument for exercise is that it takes too much time. But exercise, for the sake of enhancing our emotional state, really requires only thirty to forty minutes several times a week. We don't have to spend long hours in the gym. Some experts say that maintaining a consistent training-level heart rate for twenty-five minutes alters the brain chemistry in the same way an antidepressant does.

Since it takes a few minutes to work the heart up to a training-level pulse, I encourage my clients to set aside a minimum of thirty minutes for aerobic activity. An exercise trainer at a local club can help you calculate your training heart rate based on your age and overall physical condition.

If you are having difficulty letting go of worry and anxiety, I sincerely hope that you'll try to carve out some time in your schedule for exercise. It really doesn't matter what kind of activity you choose, as long as it's aerobic and increases your heart rate and the flow of oxygen and blood to the brain. Do something you enjoy. Walk. Ride a bike. Swim. Jog. Rollerblade. Play an intense game of basketball. Do anything that will push the tension out of your body and release those natural chemicals in the brain that can help you cope. Your proficiency on task will be much better when your mood is good, your mind is peaceful, and your body is strong. The benefits far outweigh the cost.[2]

59

Your body will never lie to you. If you feel restless or on edge and worries are keeping you up at night, pay attention to your physical needs. To improve your sleep you might want to consider some of the following suggestions:

- Don't drink caffeine or eat foods containing caffeine (chocolate) within six hours of bedtime.
- Don't use decongestants within six hours of bedtime. A twenty-four-hour, time-release decongestant can interrupt your sleep. Antihistamines are a good alternative at night because they tend to cause drowsiness.
- Don't drink alcohol within four to six hours of bedtime. Although it may initially make you drowsy, it can disrupt sound sleep.
- Don't exercise within four hours of bedtime. The hormones released in the brain during exercise can interrupt sleep. Optimum sleep seems to occur when exercise is done approximately six hours before going to bed.
- Take a hot bath or try some other relaxing activity during the hour before bedtime to allow the body to calm down naturally.

- Sip a soothing herbal tea while reading a good book in a quiet, comfortable place.

If you try doing these things, yet find that you are still not able to sleep well, I encourage you to consult your doctor. Some physicians suggest trying an antihistamine at bedtime to help induce sleep. Other nonhabit-forming medications can help break a pattern of insomnia and get you back on track. You might also want to talk with a trained nutritionist about using vitamin and mineral supplements. A number of herbs, such as valerian root, kava kava, and chamomile, are known to calm the central nervous system.

Small adjustments can make a big difference. Even if you increase your sleep by only thirty minutes a night, your brain will reward you with improved functioning. I think there's a lot of common sense in the old saying: The more you sleep, the less you'll worry.

So here's what I want you to do,

God helping you:

Take your everyday, ordinary life—

your sleeping, eating, going-to-work,

and walking-around life—

and place it before God as an offering.

ROMANS 12:1, THE MESSAGE

REASSURE

YOURSELF

I HAVE A QUESTION FOR YOU: WHAT DO YOU THINK IS THE most frequent instruction God gives to the human race? Would you say that it's to love one another, to love God, not to sin, or not to be afraid? If you chose the last option, you're right. Three hundred sixty-five verses in the Bible address our fears, anxieties, and worries. That's one golden nugget for each day of the year. God knows our frailties. He understands our tendency to fret, and time and again He offers us reassurance.

I've heard people say, "I wouldn't be so worried and anxious if I didn't have this big problem." The underlying assumption is that the situation they are facing is producing their anxiety. I'm not so sure. If that's the case, why can two people in the same situation have totally different responses? Why does one person feel panic when another feels peace? Why do some exhibit worry, anxiety, and even terror, while others exude confidence and bold courage? Let's consider a couple of situations where we find opposite responses to the same threatening circumstances.

When Moses sent scouts to explore the Promised Land, he ordered twelve of his brightest and best-trained warriors to spy out the enemy territory and report back to him (Numbers 13–14). When they returned, ten of the scouts told Moses that the land was rich and fertile. Without a doubt, it was the best piece of real estate around. But they were terrified of the people who lived there. "They are too strong for us!" they cried. "They're giants! We are like grasshoppers compared to them! We'll never conquer them!"

63

But two of the soldiers, Joshua and Caleb, had a very different response. They looked at the same land, saw the same towering giants, and told Moses, "The land is awesome and our enemies are huge, but we will certainly conquer them with God's help." Ten responded with panic, two with peace.

[The Lord said,] "Be strong and courageous.
Do not be terrified; do not be discouraged,
for the Lord your God will be
with you wherever you go."

JOSHUA 1:9

Then there's the well-known story of David and Goliath (1 Samuel 17). One afternoon, Jesse, David's father, called the young boy in from tending sheep and asked him to deliver some supplies to his brothers, who were serving in Israel's army. Toting a bundle of food under his arm, David made the trek to the Valley of Elah, where the Israelites were encamped on a hill opposite the army of the Philistines.

Every day, Goliath, the Philistines' champion, stood on the plain in the valley, mocking God and daring anyone from Israel's army to fight him. Every day for forty days no one had accepted his challenge. Everyone knew that it was a suicide mission. Goliath was too big, too formidable a foe.

It's no wonder. Goliath came from Gath, the part of the Promised Land known as the "land of the giants"—the same region Moses' scouts had spied out. Of all the giants in the land, Goliath, who stood about nine feet seven inches tall, was the biggest of all. And his weapons were just as intimidating as his size. He carried a javelin as big as a weaver's beam, with an iron point that weighed about twenty-five pounds. His spear was like a small telephone pole with a twenty-five-pound, razor-sharp arrow on the end. His coat of armor weighed nearly two hundred pounds. Scholars have calculated that in order to be mobile while wearing this weighty armor, Goliath must have weighed between four hundred and five hundred pounds, with about one percent body fat.

When David walked into camp on the forty-first day, Goliath was in the middle of the field screaming blasphemies and strutting his seven hundred pounds of muscle and metal, while the Israelites stood motionless and terrified. Except David. He surprised everyone. He marched into the valley, pausing just long enough to pick up five stones and put one of them in his sling. Then he ran full speed ahead at Goliath. You know the rest of the story: With one little stone, David slew the giant.

Thousands of people lined both sides of the valley that day, and all they could see was Goliath. He was so big and so intimidating that they couldn't take their eyes off of him. David saw what everyone else saw that day, and yet he was fearless when others were shaking in their boots. What made the difference? What gave him confidence and courage?

David's words to Goliath reveal the source of the young man's strength:

> "You come against me with sword and spear and javelin, but I come against you in the name of the LORD Almighty, the God of the armies of Israel, whom you have defied. This day the LORD will hand you over to me, and I'll strike you down and cut off your head.... And the whole world will know that there is a God in Israel. All those gathered here will know that it is not by sword or spear that the LORD saves; for the battle is the LORD's, and he will give all of you into our hands."
>
> 1 SAMUEL 17:45-47

The first stone David slung at Goliath was not one he picked up off the ground; it was the truth about God. David knew that God is all-powerful and that He was on his side. That truth steadied him. His confidence didn't come from analyzing, assessing, or running calculations. He didn't spend his mental energy on "what ifs" or evaluating whether or not he had the resources necessary to win the battle. His mind wasn't on any of those things. It was on God and His ability.[1]

*The knowledge that we are never
alone calms the troubled sea of our lives
and speaks peace to our souls.*

A. W. TOZER

Like David, when towering giants suddenly appear on the horizon of our lives, we need reassurance that God is mighty on our behalf. That means reminding ourselves that the same God who spoke the universe into existence can create something out of nothing in whatever problematic situation we're facing. It means reassuring ourselves that the same God that David boasted of more than two thousand years ago is eager to help us slay the giants that have us shaking in our boots. One of the nicest gifts we can give ourselves when we're facing threatening situations is to remind ourselves that God is with us and that everything is going to be all right. When it's all said and done, He has the final say. This is not blind optimism, naïveté, or a Pollyanna approach to life. It's a fact, based on the truth about God as He has revealed Himself to mankind.

*We impoverish God's ministry
to us the moment we forget he is Almighty;
the impoverishment is in us, not in him.*

OSWALD CHAMBERS

May I offer you some truths to sling at your own personal giants? Try pulling a few of these stones out of your pocket the next time worry has you shaking in your boots.

- "The LORD is close to the brokenhearted and saves those who are crushed in spirit" (Psalm 34:18). When you feel defeated, beaten down by life, and worried that you don't have what it takes to endure, remember this truth: You may not have what you need, but God does, and He promises to stick close to your side and see you through. He will be your champion and companion in your suffering.
- "The LORD will fight for you while you keep silent" (Exodus 14:14, NASB). When you are treated unjustly or unfairly accused, God will be your defense. He will fight for you. Be still. Keep your mouth closed and your eyes open. Watch Him act on your behalf.
- "Jesus...said, 'With man this is impossible, but with God all things are possible'" (Matthew 19:26). When you see no way, God will make one. It's not up to you; it's up to Him.
- "Even though I walk through the valley of the shadow of death, I will fear no evil, for you are with me.... Surely goodness and love will follow me all the days of my life" (Psalm 23:4, 6). When you are riddled with worry or anxiety, you can reassure yourself that God is good. His goodness and love will continue to unfold in your life now and in the future.

- "[Be] confident of this, that he who began a good work in you will carry it on to completion" (Philippians 1:6). Even though you might not have a clue about what's going on in your life, God sees the whole picture. He knows what He is doing, and it is a good work. Be confident that He hasn't brought you this far just to leave you hanging. Reassure yourself that God will accomplish what concerns you.

- "I will instruct you and teach you in the way you should go; I will counsel you and watch over you" (Psalm 32:8). You have the wisest Guide in the universe to lead you. When you are worried about making a good decision, God will instruct you. He knows every pro and con of every option you're considering. Ask Him for wisdom. Reassure yourself that God always has your best interest at heart and that He will never steer you in a wrong direction.

- "Now to him [God] who is able to do immeasurably more than all we ask or imagine, according to his power that is at work within us, to him be glory" (Ephesians 3:20–21). You have never prayed a prayer that matches God's power. You have never asked for anything that has fully tapped God's capabilities. Let your imagination run wild with that idea for a moment. Then ask.

- "But I trust in you, O LORD; I say, 'You are my God.' My times are in your hands" (Psalm 31:14–15). When you're anxious about the timing of something important to you, reassure yourself that God is overseeing every detail of your life. He is never in a hurry and never late. Relax in His timing. Events will unfold according to His plan.

Confidence. Boldness. Courage. Freedom from worry and anxiety. David had all those things when he squared off against Goliath in the Valley of Elah. They can be yours, too, when you reassure yourself with truth. Remember, your perspective determines whether you will experience panic or peace. When you keep God in your sights, your courage soars, and you can face your worries and anxieties and let them go.

69

Victory is won not in miles but in inches.
Win a little now, hold your ground,
and later win a little more.

LOUIS L'AMOUR

CHAPTER EIGHT

REDUCE
STIMULATION

I WAS SICK WITH THE FLU, LAID OUT FLAT IN BED. MY STOMACH was sour, my body ached, and I felt downright awful. I tried to prop myself up to read, but my head started spinning, and my eyes didn't want to focus on the words in front of me. Setting the book aside, I resumed a horizontal position, grabbed the remote, and flipped on the TV. The morning news was in full swing, and I figured a little diversion from my aches and pains would help.

Ten minutes later I felt worse. The news anchors bombarded me with one horrific story after another. Shooting here. Major car wreck there. Earthquake here. Plane crash there. Robbery here. Lead poisoning and cancer-causing agents there. One thing's for sure: The media work hard to emotionally hook the viewing audience. They love to hype tragedies and deliver stories with intense emotional impact. The more traumatic the event and sensational the commentary, the better. *Enough already!* The program created more anxiety than it was worth. I turned off the television, threw the covers over my head, and decided to sleep things off.

When you're enduring a stressful time in life, your emotions already tend to be more "charged" than when life is going smoothly. Your nerves might feel raw. Adding more negative stimulation to the equation is not going to lead you to inner peace. If you find yourself struggling with worry and anxiety, you might want to evaluate the sources of stimulation you are exposed to on a regular basis. Some of these sources may be intensifying your anxiety.

True silence is the rest of the mind,
and is to the spirit what sleep is to the body,
nourishment and refreshment.

WILLIAM PENN

For the first few months following the death of our first baby, I was emotionally ravaged by grief and worried that we wouldn't be able to have children. The stress of the loss and the hormonal changes in my body left me feeling very fragile. Prior to the loss of our baby, my husband and I had routinely read the newspaper in the morning before work and watched the news at the end of the day. After the baby died, though, I couldn't watch movies, listen to songs, or sit through television programs heavily laden with intense emotional content. The excessive stimulation tied my stomach in knots. I simply did not have the emotional stamina to metabolize that much bad news all at once. Grief has a way of distorting our perception. Everything already seems bad, and piling more bad on top of what already seems bad just makes us feel worse.

For several months I carefully selected what I listened

to, read, and viewed. I skipped the newspaper and chose more uplifting reading material. Though I didn't like the idea of being less in touch with what was going on in the world, I did enjoy more peace of mind. Instrumental music with soothing harmonies also had a calming effect on my emotions.

74

Positive input from the outside helped to calm my turmoil on the inside and fortified me to do the grief work I needed to do. These simple adjustments didn't remove the pain of our loss, but they markedly reduced the worry and anxiety evoked by the grief process.

Man's world has become a nervous one,

encompassed by anxiety.

God's world is other than this;

always balanced, calm, and in order.

FAITH BALDWIN

As I've worked with people in my counseling office during the last decade, I've noticed a new trend that has the potential of perpetuating anxiety. More and more I'm meeting clients who spend the entire evening after work, or after the kids are in bed, on the Internet.

For those who are somewhat socially anxious, being online can seem a safer place to interact with others. There is no face-to-face contact, and if they don't want to continue interacting with someone, they can click off-line with one push of a button.

Please don't get me wrong. I use the Internet regularly for a variety of purposes. It's a wonderful tool. But problems arise when the Net becomes a person's main source of relationship or when the stimulating impact of the activity robs him or her of sleep or interaction with family members and friends.

Virtual friendships cannot meet our needs for healthy human connection because much of what is perceived on-line is only a small portion of reality—the reality the other person wants you to see in the written word—not the complete picture of who he or she actually *is*.

I've met men and women who were duped into thinking they had met Prince Charming or Miss Perfect in chat rooms on-line. It was a heartbreaking and rude awakening when they eventually found out that they had wasted hours, even months, of their lives on some fanciful illusion presented in text. Worse yet, I've talked with clients who unwittingly interacted with smooth-talking users and abusers. What started as an innocent conversation in a chat room led to a scary and troublesome series of events. I don't want to be a gloom-and-doomer, but I do want to suggest exercising healthy caution and setting time limits for on-line interactions.

Research supports the importance of using the Internet wisely. I recently read a study funded by a group of computer companies. Researchers went to a town in Pennsylvania and selected two thousand homes that did not have Internet access. The families who agreed to participate in the study were given a computer and Internet access in exchange for the researchers' right to study them for two years.

At the beginning and end of the test period the

participants took a psychological test. I don't think the computer companies expected the results they received. At the end of two years, the study revealed that those individuals who spent more than one hour on-line per day were significantly more depressed than before they had access to the Internet.[1]

We don't have to take an all-or-nothing approach. Balance is the key. When we're living with a heightened sense of anxiety, we need to take inventory of what is assaulting our senses. Sometimes we use the media and computers as diversions to escape from our worries. But if we are being bombarded with toxic and emotionally intense messages, or the time we spend in these activities is robbing us of needed rest or time with loved ones, we might actually be making our problems worse.

A wise old sage by the name of Peter once wrote, "Whoever would love life and see good days…must seek peace and pursue it" (1 Peter 3:10–11). Are you up for a challenge? Even small adjustments that reduce stimulation can have a positive emotional impact and diminish your worries. Why not give it a try? Quiet some of that outside noise for a week or two, and see if your world seems like a more enjoyable place to live. See if peace doesn't follow your pursuit and help you let go of some of your anxiety.

It is in lonely solitude that God delivers his best thoughts, and the mind needs to be still and quiet to receive them.

CHARLES SWINDOLL

CHAPTER NINE

ROCK

WITH

LAUGHTER

WHEN WAS THE LAST TIME YOU HAD A GOOD, SOLID, BELLY laugh—you know, the kind that leaves you gasping for air? Did you know that laughter is a medicine for the soul? It can promote sound mental and physical health, deflect anxious thoughts, and help us cope more effectively with overwhelming pressures. Laughter has an amazing power to balance our steps as we walk the tightrope of life.

Medical researchers have discovered that laughter actually stimulates the immune system. It also increases our oxygen intake, lowers blood pressure, and releases endorphins in the pleasure center of the brain, giving us an emotional lift or natural high, regardless of whatever anxiety-producing circumstances we may be enduring.

My friend Bonnie Kopp recently endured a year filled with the natural worry and anxiety that accompanies a diagnosis of breast cancer. But in the midst of some very long and trying months, Bonnie and her twin sister, Connie Griffith, decided to have some fun.

During their teenage years, Bonnie and Connie were known for pulling "twin switches": On double dates they would swap clothes midway through the evening and pretend to be each other. Even their boyfriends couldn't tell them apart! Now in their fifties, the twins continue their humorous shenanigans. After a visit from this dynamic duo, the radiology lab at Emanuel Hospital has never been the same. I'm going to let Bonnie tell you the story firsthand.

A cheerful heart is good medicine,
but a broken spirit saps a person's strength.

PROVERBS 17:22, NLT

After I was diagnosed with breast cancer, I received radiation treatment five days a week for six weeks. About midway through the process, Connie called to say that she was going to pass through town for a brief visit on her way to an overseas assignment in India. This would be the last chance I'd have to see her for a very long time.

The circumstances were less than ideal. I was extremely fatigued from the radiation and a bit discouraged by the daily ordeal of having to visit the cold, sterile radiation lab. The atmosphere there was morbidly solemn; a sense of death lurked in every corner. Most of the people walking in and out of the place seemed stunned, not knowing whether they were going to live or die. The hospital personnel, who worked with dying people every day, were fairly desensitized, and whenever I arrived for my appointment, they made minimal eye contact with me. The nurses focused strictly on the task at hand, dedicating themselves to keeping the patients on schedule and the medical interventions correct.

The night Connie arrived, I felt inspired. I'd had enough gloom and doom in that radiation lab. It was time to liven up the atmosphere and give those nurses a shot of good ol' down-to-earth fun. I concocted a plan and asked Connie if she would be my accomplice. Usually she would have jumped at the chance to pull a twin switch, but she was a bit uncomfortable doing it to professionals and people we really didn't know. Plus, being around radiation kind of scared her. But with a little cajoling on my part, she reluctantly agreed.

Humor makes all things tolerable.

HENRY WARD BEECHER

(Before I tell you any more, you need to know that, early in my treatment, the nurses had tattooed small dots on my chest where the radiation was to be administered. These marks are permanent. Okay, read on!)

While driving to the hospital the next morning, we asked God to please deposit some of His life and joy in that place of death. When we arrived, the nurses were busy with business behind the counter and didn't notice that two of us had entered instead of one. We went directly to the changing room, where I gave Connie my gown. Then I coached her on the procedure.

"After you change, go into the waiting area, and stay put until a nurse comes to get you. She'll take you to the radiation lab. When you get to the lab, climb up on the table, lie down, and raise your arm above your head."

Connie played along. I watched from inside the dressing room with the light off and the door slightly ajar. I wasn't about to miss seeing our scheme unfold.

A nurse arrived right on schedule and greeted Connie. "Good morning. How are you doing today?"

"Oh, it's been such a busy morning," Connie replied. "I'm feeling a little confused."

"Well, just follow me," the nurse said.

My sister hopped up on the table, lay down, and lifted her arm over her head per my instructions. But there was a problem. The next thing Connie heard was, "My goodness. You *are* confused! Your head is at the wrong end of the table!"

Connie was so rattled by the obvious mistake that her hands began to tremble, making it hard for her to undo her gown for the next step in the treatment. The nurse was quick to pick up on it. "You're not only confused," she exclaimed; "you're nervous!"

Playing along, Connie said, "I just don't know what's wrong with me. I'm obviously not myself today."

Laughter is a tranquilizer with no side effects.
ARNOLD GLASGOW

Next the nurse needed to align the beams of light with the tattoos. But the marks were nowhere to be found. The nurse shrieked, "There are no tattoos!"

One of the other nurses, who had been working in the lab for more than five years, came running. "I've never seen anything like this before!" she exclaimed.

The two of them carefully searched for the dots. They paused only to look at each other with eyes the size of golf balls.

About that time I very nonchalantly walked out of the dressing room and asked the staff in a stern tone of voice: "What are you doing, giving radiation to the wrong patient?"

The technician almost fainted, and one of the nurses screamed, "There are two of you!" The rest of the staff erupted into such hilarious laughter that they could hardly catch their breath.

After the laughter subsided, I switched places with Connie and, sure enough, the dots were right where they had been the day before. I continued with treatment while Connie changed her clothes and took a seat in the waiting room.

A man who was waiting for his wife wanted to know what all the laughter in the other room was about, and Connie told him the story. Guffawing, he was almost falling out of his chair when his wife walked in. This piqued her curiosity, and she, too, wanted an explanation. When Connie told her what we had done, she doubled over in laughter. Then Connie noticed tears streaming down the husband's face. When he finally regained his composure, he hugged his wife tightly and said to Connie in a shaking voice, "Thank you. Thank you for doing this. My wife thinks she is dying, and this is the first time I've seen her laugh in three months."

The doctor administering my treatment turned to me and said, "You brought more healing today than any radiation ever could. Thank you for being brave enough to pull the switch—and for giving everyone a good, hard laugh!"[1]

❧

A sense of humor can help you overlook the unattractive, tolerate the unpleasant, cope with the unexpected, and smile through the unbearable.

MOSHE WALDOKS

I love the twins' lighthearted spunk. It just goes to show you that a little levity can help blow your cares away.

Does something seem terribly important today? Are you distracted by anxieties that won't give you a moment of peace? Try to look for the funny side of life. And remember: Some things that seem terribly important and serious now might become absolutely hilarious after a little time passes.

He who laughs, lasts.

REFUSE TO ASSUME THE WORST

SOMETIMES WE FRIGHTEN OURSELVES WITH OUR OWN thoughts. Our mind locks on an ordinary concern, stews on it a while, and then, before we know it, turns the problem into a horrible tragedy. In the counseling office we call this not-so-wonderful talent "catastrophizing."

After any situation in which our mind is overtaxed for a prolonged period of time, our psychological defenses are weak, and we find it difficult to ward off worries. Anxious thoughts that typically would bounce off of us during less stressful times seem to penetrate and stick. Once they stick, they grow, and we lose an accurate perspective of what is really happening.

One of the best ways to manage worries that are multiplying exponentially is simply to interrupt the process in your head by saying firmly, "Stop it!" Assertively halt the escalating thoughts.

I remember well the week after I came home from the hospital following Nathan's birth. Grieving his Down syndrome and worried about the holes in his heart, I was in a dark funk. One afternoon John was home sick with the flu, and I was doing what

I could to keep plenty of liquids and pain relievers handy for him. When I walked downstairs to our family room to give him some chicken noodle soup, I saw that he was sleeping. Something about the way he was lying there triggered my memory of seeing John's father in an open casket during his memorial service, and the thought shot through my mind: *It's probably some fatal illness, and John's going to die, too.* Anxiety roared.

I shook my head in frustration, fully aware that the thought was irrational. "Stop it!" I blurted out. "This is ridiculous!"

My words startled John. In a flash he sat bolt upright and shouted, "What? What?"

His reaction scared me silly and I screamed back, "What? What?"

And the soup? Well, let's just say it never made it to its intended destination.

We both burst out laughing when we realized what had happened. And you know what? When the gloomy thoughts stopped, my anxiety faded.

When we fuel our fears by catastrophizing, we actually create mental anguish and become our own worst enemy. The good news is that we don't have to compulsively follow every train of thought that enters our head. A thought is simply a thought. We don't have to give it more power than it deserves.

Worry gives a small thing a big shadow.

SWEDISH PROVERB

88

In refusing to assume the worst, it helps if we give our scary predictions a reality check. I recently had a front-row seat watching Bill, a business executive, do this in the corporate world. After a number of his associates lost their positions due to a company merger, Bill made an appointment with me for some help in learning how to work with what he called "off-the-chart anxiety."

The last few months had been extremely stressful for those in the company's higher management positions. Bill wasn't sleeping well, and he felt as if he had to walk on pins and needles at the office. No one knew from one day to the next who might get the axe. Rumors flew. Some were founded on partial truth; others were gross exaggerations.

The blood draining from his face, Bill told me: "I knew I was in trouble when my boss passed me in the hall and didn't even acknowledge me."

"Did he see you when you passed each other?" I asked.

"He couldn't have missed me," he replied. "There were just two of us in the hallway."

Bill went on to discuss some of the office politics involved and the reasons why he believed he would be laid off. "I think my boss is avoiding me because he knows I'm the next to go. I can feel it coming."

I do believe there are times when we can intuitively sense that something is coming down the pike, but my gut told me that Bill's anxiety, not the gift of discernment, was driving his impressions. His conclusion was natural for a mind riddled with worry.

Bill had not spoken to his boss since that troublesome

day when they had silently passed each other in the hallway. I suggested that he test his fear against reality by scheduling an appointment with his boss as soon as possible. The unknowns were giving too much room for speculation. Bill's goal was to check out his impressions.

Two weeks later Bill returned. He had had a long discussion with his boss about the company merger, and in that meeting he saw a whole new side of his boss. Clarity came. When his boss identified him as "a key contributor with a bright future," Bill knew that he had confidence in him. He realized that his earlier impressions had been far off the mark. They were irrational fears fueled by the stressful changes on the job and his chronic fatigue.

When I asked Bill about the incident in the hallway, he shrugged it off, saying that his boss probably hadn't seen him because he was preoccupied. It was a healthy perspective coming from a peaceful mind.

When we're worried and anxious, our imaginations can run wild. And the more they do, the more anxious we feel. It's a vicious spiral. But the spiral can be easily interrupted. We can say *stop* to our thoughts. We can test reality and refuse to let little things become big things. If you want to let go of worry and anxiety, remind yourself: *This problem doesn't have to be a big deal. I don't have to blow things out of proportion.* A pebble is a pebble, not a boulder. A speed bump is a speed bump, not an impenetrable concrete wall. A concern is a concern, not a major disaster. A temporary setback is just that, not a permanent failure cast in stone for all of eternity. Keep that in mind the next time you start to assume the worst.

Fear.

His modus operandi is to manipulate
you with the mysterious,
to taunt you with the unknown.
Fear of death, fear of failure, fear of God,
fear of tomorrow—his arsenal is vast.
His goal? To create cowardly, joyless souls.
He doesn't want you to make
the journey to the mountain.
He figures if he can rattle you enough,
you will take your eyes off the peaks
and settle for a dull existence in the flatlands.

MAX LUCADO

CHAPTER ELEVEN

RELY ON FAITH

A wise man once said,

"Whatever came to me, I looked on it as

God's gift for some special purpose.

If it was a difficulty,

I knew He gave it to me to struggle with,

to strengthen my mind and my faith."

That idea has sweetened and helped me all of my life.

ANONYMOUS

THOUGH WE LIVE IN A WORLD FILLED WITH UNEXPECTED problems, unpredictable outcomes, and upsetting realities, worry and anxiety don't have to be the defining qualities of our lives. As we learn how to let go of these troubling emotions, confidence and peace of mind can govern our experiences. But these qualities don't come strictly from our own efforts; they also come as we trust. Brennan Manning, one of my favorite writers, says it well:

> Like faith and hope, trust cannot be self-generated. I cannot simply *will* myself to trust. What outrageous irony: the one thing I am responsible for throughout my life I cannot generate. The one thing I need to do I cannot do. But such is the meaning of radical dependence. It consists in theological virtues, in divinely ordained gifts.[1]

One morning shortly after Nathan was born, I came across a passage in the Bible that spoke of these divinely ordained gifts. I had read these paragraphs many times before, but on that particular morning the words carried new meaning for me:

> Now there are different kinds of spiritual gifts, but it is the same Holy Spirit who is the source of them all.... A spiritual gift is given to each of us as a means of helping the entire church.
>
> To one person the Spirit gives the ability to give wise advice; to another he gives the gift of special knowledge. The Spirit gives special faith to another, and to someone else he gives the power to heal the sick.... It is the one and only Holy Spirit who distributes these gifts.
>
> I CORINTHIANS 12:4, 7–9, 11, NLT

I already knew that I had a measure of faith. But these verses talk about a special spiritual gift of faith imparted by the Spirit of God that goes beyond the norm. In this context, it's a faith that enables a person to be fully persuaded by and completely reliant on the truthfulness of God. It is faith that facilitates trust.

I want this, Lord! I exclaimed to myself. *Worries are getting the best of me. I need Your Spirit to give me faith. It says here that You give special faith to some. I want all You have to give, Lord.*

I can't tell you that all my fears dissolved with that brief prayer, but I can tell you that I began to sense a greater propensity in my spirit to believe God for whatever I needed at any given time. As I continued to replenish my spirit and open my heart to the Lord, my anxiety became more manageable. In the process, it became very clear to me that faith and fear are powerful opposites. Faith doesn't necessarily make all of our fears disappear, but it does empower us to be people of courage who can tolerate distress and cope with life's hardships.

Earlier in this book I mentioned an acrostic for the word *fear*: False Evidence Appearing Real. I decided to develop an acrostic for the word *faith* to use when I was caught in the crossfire of scary thoughts: Fully Abandoned (to God) In Trust (and) Humility. When I'm facing trials and tribulations and I'm vulnerable to those gnawing "what ifs," I need to activate my faith. I need to tilt my head heavenward, raise my hands in surrender, and say, *God, no matter what, I am fully abandoned to You in trust and humility.*

This was a posture I sensed in a man whose faith caused Jesus to marvel. You can read about him in the book of Matthew:

> When Jesus had entered Capernaum, a centurion came to him, asking for help. "Lord," he said, "my servant lies at home paralyzed and in terrible suffering."
>
> Jesus said to him, "I will go and heal him."
>
> The centurion replied, "Lord, I do not deserve to have you come under my roof. But just say the word, and my servant will be

healed. For I myself am a man under authority, with soldiers under me. I tell this one, 'Go,' and he goes; and that one, 'Come,' and he comes. I say to my servant, 'Do this,' and he does it."

When Jesus heard this, he *was astonished* and said to those following him, "I tell you the truth, I have not found anyone in Israel with such great faith."

Then Jesus said to the centurion, "Go! It will be done just as you believed it would." And his servant was healed at that very hour.

Matthew 8:5–10, 13, emphasis mine

I read this story through several times and wondered what Jesus saw in this man's heart. He wasn't a religious leader. He wasn't even a Jew. He was a Roman soldier. Think about it: For years Jesus had mixed with the most religious people of His day. He had rubbed shoulders with prominent Old Testament scholars. He had personally trained and mentored a select few. But these verses say that Jesus had not met anyone in Israel with such astounding faith.

Do you know that there are only two places in the Bible where Jesus is amazed at anything? One is in this text. The other is where Jesus marvels at the unbelief of the people in His hometown.

I searched the story to find out why the man had received such an accolade. He doesn't appear to have done anything. Jesus' disciples had been performing mind-boggling miracles among the crowds, yet the Lord didn't single out any of them as having tremendous faith. What did Jesus see in this soldier?

I think one answer lies in the soldier's response to Jesus. The story says that this Roman soldier called him "Lord." That may not seem like a big deal to you, but back then it was politically incorrect—a full-fledged no-no! Understanding the historical context is critical.

From numerous records we know that at the time all Roman citizens were required to revere the emperor as their lord. Anything to the contrary invited severe punishment. This Roman soldier was well aware of the laws of the day. After all, he helped the emperor enforce them. He knew that when he publicly addressed Jesus as "Lord," he was risking his life. Punishment for this infraction ranged from loss of rank to execution.

This particular Roman soldier was an officer of high rank who had trained and worked diligently for years to attain his status. Now he was wealthy and powerful. Yet with a few public words about Jesus, he risked losing everything, including his life. The soldier's comment demonstrated total abandonment, complete trust, and absolute humility before the One he addressed as "Lord."[2]

Scores of people stood around Jesus and the soldier that day. Many believed that Jesus could work miracles. But those seeking only the miraculous didn't impress Him. Instead, He marveled at a man who, through enormous faith, was willing to trust Him with everything.

What the story of the Roman soldier says to me is that God doesn't want first place in my life; He wants all of my life. He wants me to abandon myself totally to Him. He wants me to confidently, actively believe in His ability to care for me.

Brennan Manning describes this attitude of the heart beautifully:

> Abba, into your hands I entrust my body, mind, and spirit and this entire day—morning, afternoon, evening, and night. Whatever you want of me, I want of me, falling into you and trusting you in the midst of my life. Into your heart I entrust my heart, feeble, distracted, insecure, uncertain. God, unto you I abandon myself in Jesus our Lord. Amen.[3]

This is the attitude we need when we are suffering hardship or emerging from the shadows of a dark time of stress, our confidence shaken. Overwhelming pressures can break down our defenses and create a crisis of faith. When we're flooded with anxiety, we can find ourselves asking questions that would otherwise be unthinkable:

Where is God?

Does God love me?

Is God really in control?

How can anything good possibly come out of something so bad?

Anxiety distorts our perception. Worry burns up a tremendous amount of mental and emotional energy. If you have recently suffered from worry and anxiety, please give yourself grace. Give yourself time to process your thoughts and feelings. And give God time to restore your bearings.

It has been almost a decade since Nathan entered this

world. I still frequently ask God to grant me the gift of faith. Every now and then anxiety still gets the best of me, but over time it has subsided. The practice of surrendering to His ways and purposes is becoming more habitual. When worries surface, prompting me to forecast negatively, I calm myself down by making statements of faith.

Remember, the battle of faith against fear is waged in the mind. Fearful thoughts agitate the body. Faith-filled thoughts bring peace. I'll show you what I mean.

When you're in the middle of adversity:
Fear says, "God has left you. He doesn't care.
You're on your own."
Faith says, "In God's kingdom everything
is based on promise, not on feeling.
God has a plan, and it is built on love."

When someone has ripped you off:
Fear says, "You can't trust people."
Faith says, "God, the Redeemer, restores stolen goods
to their rightful owners, one way or another."

When you're slandered:
Fear says, "Everyone is talking.
Your reputation is smeared for life."
Faith says, "God will straighten the record
when false things have been said about me."

When you've made a major blunder:
Fear says, "It's over. You've blown it.
You may as well throw in the towel."
Faith says, "Failure is always an event, never a person.
God will use my strengths and my weaknesses
to accomplish His plans."

When you're waiting for something:
Fear says, "You're going to be on hold forever."
Faith says, "My time is in God's hands.
He will accomplish His plans for me right on schedule."

When you ask God for something, and He says no:
Fear says, "If God really loved you,
He would give you what you want."
Faith says, "God is acting for my highest good."

When you fail:
Fear says, "You can't trust God.
Look at how He's let you down."
Faith says, "God has proven His trustworthiness
by dying for me."

When you're staggering under a load of guilt:
Fear says, "Your mistakes will haunt you the rest of your life."
Faith says, "God holds nothing against me.
He has sovereignly declared me pardoned."

When you face stinging regret:
Fear says, "Your scars limit you."
Faith says, "I am useful to God not in spite of my scars,
but because of them."

When a friend has let you down:
Fear says, "Why bother? It's not worth going on."
Faith says, "God will take the wrongs others have done me
and use them for my ultimate good."

When you experience the pruning of God's shears:
Fear says, "If God loved you, He wouldn't
let you suffer like this."
Faith says, "God knows what I need better than I do.
Even Christ learned obedience through what He suffered."

Friend, our worries and anxieties don't intimidate God. Nor do our feelings influence God's responses.

But our faith does.

Let's allow our anxieties to be a reminder of our need to surrender—to abandon ourselves fully to God in trust and humility. Let's use worry to trigger a prayer:

God, please birth the gift of faith in my spirit
today. Help me to believe in ways I have not yet
believed. Exchange my spirit of fear for a spirit
of faith. Open the eyes of my heart to see the

differences the gifts of Your Spirit are making in
my life—today.

On the heels of that kind of prayer, I think we may give
the Lord some more opportunities to marvel.[4]

101

Biographies of bold disciples
begin with chapters of honest terror.
Fear of death. Fear of failure.
Fear of loneliness. Fear of a wasted life....
Faith begins when you see God on the mountain
and you are in the valley and you know
that you're too weak to make the climb.
You see what you need...you see what you have...
and it isn't enough....
But He is!... Faith that begins with
fear will end up nearer the Father.

MAX LUCADO

RELAX

YOUR

GRIP

IF YOU READ MY FIRST BOOK IN THIS SERIES, *Letting Go of Disappointments and Painful Losses,* you might remember an exercise I suggested. It goes like this: Clench your fist into a ball. Squeeze as hard as you can, and count to ten. Study your hand as you do so.

Ready? Go. S-q-u-e-e-e-e-z-e.

Okay, now relax. How did your fist feel, gripping so tightly? What did it look like? Can you describe the sensations you felt? How did it feel to release your grip and open your hand after you counted to ten?

When your hand was clenched, it was uncomfortable, wasn't it? Tense. Bloodless. Unable to move freely. Not only that, but it wasn't able to do what it was *designed* to do. Your hand was closed, unable to receive. But when you let go and opened your hand, you could feel the blood returning to your fingers, couldn't you? Your hand became warm again. It relaxed, the discomfort left, and you felt relief. Your fingers moved naturally, and your hand was in a much better position to receive.

There are similarities between our physical bodies and our psyches. When we go through life grasping, clinging, clutching, and desperately trying to hang on to things that should naturally be released, we ache. We get tied up in knots. We become emotionally constricted and locked up in pain. We lose freedom of movement in our lives and feel paralyzed.[1]

Sometimes we hang on tight to our worries in a superstitious sort of way. We think that somehow we will be able to prevent a negative outcome by worrying. It's as if worry had some sort of mysterious merit. I see this in people I counsel, and as irrational as I know this line of reasoning to be, I see it in my own life.

For several years during spring break, our family traveled to Mexico to help a few church congregations. John and I offered leadership training, counseling, and teaching, while our children shared skits, music, and mimes with the Hispanic children. These annual mission trips were usually wonderful weeks of work and fun, but one year held some surprises that raised my anxiety quotient to a very uncomfortable level.

Twice while we were traveling in the twelve-passenger van, we barely escaped a head-on collision. The first time, we were barreling sixty-five miles an hour down a long, steep hill when a huge bus attempted to pass a slow string of cars on the upgrade. The bus entered our lane traveling sixty miles an hour. There were no shoulders on the road, just jagged cliffs on both sides, so we couldn't pull over. John slammed on the brakes, and the bus came within inches of us before passing the other cars and switching lanes. A big delivery truck did the same thing a few days later, and again we narrowly escaped with our lives.

My worry factor ratcheted up another notch one evening when Nathan decided to play hide-and-seek without telling anyone. Just before dark our whole family, and everyone else who was sitting poolside at the hotel, ended up searching the grounds for "the little blond-haired boy with Down syndrome." I was worried that Nathan had left the hotel commons and was wandering the streets. *Safe* is not a word I would use to describe the surrounding area for an eight-year-old child on the loose. The hotel manager told us that the police probably wouldn't be any help and to "keep looking."

In the middle of our frantic search, our older son, Benjamin, ran up to our living quarters to get a bird's-eye view from the balcony. He yelled Nathan's name, and much to his surprise, Nathan answered. When Ben turned in the direction of his voice, he saw Nathan on the balcony next to ours, hiding under the patio table. He smiled and waved, as if to say, "Tag—you're it!" While we were all very relieved to find him safe and sound, I pumped so much adrenaline in those thirty minutes that three hours later I still felt weak in the knees.

An anxious heart weighs a man down.

PROVERBS 12:25

I had accepted an invitation to speak at a women's conference at Mt. Hermon, California, and was scheduled to catch a plane out of Mexico a couple of days ahead of the rest of the family. Wanting to make the most of my last morning on the Baja, I set my alarm early so I could take a long walk on the beach at sunrise. As I strolled the sandy shoreline, I prayed and reflected on the week. The night before had been one of the highlights of the trip. John and I had spoken to a very enthusiastic crowd and then had the joy of praying with many people at the close of the meeting. One of the women stood out in my mind.

Her name was Lucinda. When she approached us asking for prayer, she was obviously in deep emotional turmoil. Her eyes were red and swollen from sobbing. Through an interpreter she told us that she wanted to give her life to God, but that years before she had been involved in a number of dark activities. She spoke of being tormented by fear and needing help to be free.

Those of us who joined hands with Lucinda for prayer got a firsthand look at God's marvelous power as He released this woman from her painful captivity. In a matter of minutes she went from being hunched over in agony to standing tall. Although mascara lines streaked her cheeks, her eyes reflected peace.

As I continued musing during my trek down the beach, gentle waves lapped up over my feet, cooling them from the heat of the sun. But for some reason, in spite of the breathtaking beauty around me, my thoughts wandered onto a negative track. The hair-raising close calls we had had in the van a few days before came flooding back. Then thoughts of Nathan's hide-and-seek game intruded, and I fretted over the possibility of its happening again. His vulnerabilities and inability to sense danger scared me. I knew that the others in the family would take good care of him after I left for the women's retreat, but knowing that I wasn't going to be with him during the next couple of days left me feeling as if I had less control.

*To be controlled by the Spirit means that we are
not controlled by what happens on the outside
but by what is happening on the inside.*

ERWIN LUTZER

As my sense of control decreased, my anxiety increased. I fretted and stewed and fretted and stewed, toxic with worry— as if my worry, in some magical way, could prevent a disaster from happening. When you think about it, it's ridiculous. Even though I'd been present with my family, I hadn't had the power to control the things that had evoked my anxiety in the first place.

So I whispered a brief prayer, asking God to deliver me from these crazy, pesky fears, just as I had seen Him deliver Lucinda from her turmoil the night before.

*Some people think God does not like to be troubled
with our constant coming and asking. The way to
trouble God is not to come at all.*

DWIGHT L. MOODY

During that hour, I walked the length of the beach, passing dozens of hotels and establishments that catered to tourists. On my way back down the strip, the thought of a piping hot, fresh-brewed cup of coffee crossed my mind. Noticing a lovely outdoor café at one of the prettiest hotels on the beach, I decided to stop and order some coffee to go. I was in my running gear and had on my baseball cap, sunglasses, and headphones—not exactly the proper attire for this classy restaurant.

When I walked up the steps, a young woman greeted me and I ordered my coffee. She sent a waiter to the kitchen to get it, turned to me, and in accented English asked, "You been out running?"

"Yes," I replied, "but I really walk more than I run."

"So, how far you walk?"

"Oh, about five or six miles," I responded. "It gives me some time to myself."

"You have kids?"

"Yes, I have three children. My husband is with them. They're all still sleeping."

"You a strong woman," she said, catching me a bit off guard.

"Oh—I don't know about that," I said, shaking my head and smiling. "I have days when I don't feel very strong." As those words slipped from my mouth, I felt a blush of embarrassment and wondered why I had said them. I'm usually not that open with strangers.

"No. No. I see God in you. You are strong!" she responded with enthusiasm.

I wondered who in the world this woman was and why she would make such a bold statement to a complete stranger. "Yes, I do have God in my heart. Do you?" I asked, curious where the conversation would lead.

"Oh, *sí, sí, sí!*" she exclaimed.

"Do you have a church that you attend?"

"*Sí, sí. El Centro de Fe.*"

"The Center of Faith?" I asked curiously. "My husband I were there last night."

It was as if someone flipped a switch. She lit up from head to toe and asked, "Did you hear the message?"

Taking off my sunglasses and headphones, I smiled and said, "My husband is John, and I'm Pam. We gave the message last night."

I thought the young woman was going to faint from excitement. Her chin almost hit the floor, and she let out a screech that turned several heads in our direction. After she settled down, she introduced herself: "Remember me? I'm Lucinda. I'm the one who is free!"

Lucinda's countenance glowed. She looked so radically different from the night before that I hadn't even recognized her. No more puffy, red eyes. No mascara smudges and smears. No remnants of the agony and pain that had been written across her face. She was electric with joy. She and I chatted a few minutes about what God had done for her. Then we hugged each other, and I paid for my coffee and left.

Amazing! I thought. *Out of the dozens of hotels on this sandy strip, I "just happened" to ask for a cup of coffee where Lucinda works. Out of the dozens of waiters and waitresses working in the bustling restaurant, Lucinda "just happened" to be the one who walked over to help me.*

Coincidence? I don't think so. I believe it was a divine setup. God wanted me to know that He was leading me. He was directing my plans. He was mindful of my worries and wanted to assure me that He was big enough to take care of every one of them.

The entire way home, I kept shaking my head, marveling over God's kindness and gentle love. He knew the heavy anxiety that weighed me down as I walked the beach that morning, and He wanted to send a very clear message: *Pam, would you please relax? Trust Me with your family. I am ordering your steps, even when you aren't aware of it. I am going before you. I am going behind you. Let go of your worries. My intention is to bless you.*

I'm a bit slow to learn at times, but this time I got it. As I sensed God extending His love to me, I relaxed the death grip on my worries and received the peace that He had wanted to give me all along.

How about you? Are you clinging to worries today? All the worrying in the world isn't going to make a positive difference in the outcome of whatever is troubling you. Toxic worry isn't magic; it's misery. It doesn't solve problems; it creates problems. It doesn't provide answers; it scrambles our radar and keeps us from receiving the answers we need.

Hanging on to worry and anxiety won't do you any good. But I know something that will. Relax your grip. Open your hand so that you can receive all that God has in store for you. He loves you. He cares about every last detail of your life. And He is more capable of meeting your deepest needs than anyone else in this universe.

If you're going to cling to something or someone, cling to God. His hand of love is extended to you. He awaits your invitation. Would you like Him to help you conquer your fears?

Do you want Him to lead you to paths of peace? If so, take His hand and hang on for all you are worth.

By the way, His companionship comes with a guarantee. When you open your heart to Him, He promises that He will never, ever let go.

112

[Jesus said,] "Are you tired? Worn out?

Burned out on religion? Come to me.

Get away with me and you'll recover your life.

I'll show you how to take a real rest.

Walk with me and work with me—watch how I do it.

Learn the unforced rhythms of grace.

I won't lay anything heavy or ill-fitting on you.

Keep company with me and

you'll learn to live freely and lightly."

MATTHEW 11:28–30, *THE MESSAGE*

GROUP

DISCUSSION

QUESTIONS

CHAPTER 1: REVIEW THE FACTS

1. The acrostic FEAR stands for False Evidence Appearing Real. What concerns tend to prompt you to forecast negatively into the future? What false evidences seem very real to you when you're worried?

2. List several facts about a situation that concerns you, and allow your group to offer perspectives you may not have considered.

3. Pray for one another, asking God to give you His perspective and wisdom about each of those situations. Gather some more facts this week, and share them with the group next week.

CHAPTER 2: REGISTER YOUR CONCERNS WITH GOD

1. Have you ever had seasons of intense stress in your life when worry and anxiety seemed overwhelming? Describe your experience to the group. What helped you cope?

2. One of the ways we can register our concerns with God is by writing them in a prayer journal, or a worry registry. I

shared an excerpt from my journal. How do you register your concerns with God? What helps or hinders you from telling Him about your worries?

3. Pray for one another, asking God to help you register your concerns with Him quickly. Get a notebook this week, and start registering your worries in the form of prayers. Share the results with the group next week.

CHAPTER 3: REQUIRE A PLAN

1. Worry tends to feed on a passive mind, and it can shift the imagination into overdrive. Describe a time when you have experienced this.

2. Developing a plan to increase your sense of control during a troubling situation can help reduce anxiety. Identify one of your worries, and allow the group to brainstorm some ideas for developing a plan.

3. Pray for one another, asking God to lead you as you develop a plan. Commit the plan to Him. Next week tell your group how things went as you implemented it.

CHAPTER 4: RECONNECT WITH THE PRESENT

1. Many of our worries come from the tendency to over-estimate the probability of a harmful event and to exaggerate its potential negative impact. Describe a recent situation where this was true for you.

2. Living in the moment, instead of in the future or the past, brings peace. Brainstorm with the group some ways to cultivate this mental discipline this week.

3. Pray for one another, asking God to enable you to live in the moment. Next week share with the group your struggles and victories with this assignment.

CHAPTER 5: REACH OUT

1. I made the statement "When we withdraw, detach, or close God and others out of our suffering, we cut off our source of life and derail our own healing." What makes it hard and/or easy for you to reach out to others?
2. Identify one situation that is driving your anxiety, and risk telling the others in your group about it.
3. Pray for one another, asking the God of All Comfort to come near. Offer love, acceptance, and support to those who have risked sharing their hearts with you.

CHAPTER 6: RESPECT YOUR NEED FOR RENEWAL

1. Anxiety drives insomnia, and insomnia drives anxiety. What have you found helpful to break this vicious cycle?
2. How are you respecting your need for renewal? What is a concrete step you can take this week to take better care of yourself? Small adjustments can make a big difference.
3. Pray for one another, asking God to show you ways to renew yourself on a daily basis and to give you the power to follow through.

CHAPTER 7: REASSURE YOURSELF

1. What is the most frequent instruction God gives the human race?
2. When towering giants suddenly appear on the horizon of

our lives, we, like David, need reassurance that God is mighty on our behalf. What stones of truth from this chapter will you fling at your giants this week? Share those applications with the group.

3. Pray for one another, asking God to give you His perspective on the things that worry you. Remember that your perspective determines whether you will experience panic or peace. Next week tell your group which perspectives ushered in relief.

CHAPTER 8: REDUCE STIMULATION

1. What kinds of stimulation in your environment induce anxiety and sap your energy?
2. How can you quiet the outside noise this week in order to calm your spirit? What adjustments can you make to decrease negative stimulation and increase positive input?
3. Pray for one another, asking God to enable you to make those adjustments and to show you other creative ways to cultivate a peaceful mind. Next week talk about the results of those adjustments.

CHAPTER 9: ROCK WITH LAUGHTER

1. What tickles your funny bone or puts a smile on your face?
2. Can you recall a situation that seemed awful at the time but now causes you to chuckle? Tell the group about it.
3. Pray for one another, asking God to give you the ability to see the funny side of life this week. Invite Him to lift a spirit of heaviness from you and replace it with a spirit of joy. Next week share something that brought you joy during the week.

CHAPTER 10: REFUSE TO ASSUME THE WORST

1. Sometimes we frighten ourselves with our own thoughts. Do you ever find yourself catastrophizing? Tell the group about a time you did this.

2. There are two tools that can help us not to assume the worst. We can say, "Stop!" to our thoughts, and we can test their reality. Identify one of your worries, and then consider a way you can test the reality of your thoughts. Share your plan with the group.

3. Pray for one another, asking God to strengthen you to resist the tendency to assume the worst. Ask Him to help you find creative ways to test your thoughts against reality and to speak to you through people and situations as you search for answers. Next week share how things went as you used these tools.

CHAPTER 11: RELY ON FAITH

1. The acrostic FAITH stands for Fully Abandoned to God In Trust and Humility. What meaning could this have in relation to the anxiety-producing situations you are facing?

2. I listed a number of statements contrasting faith with fear. Choose one or two of the faith statements that were relevant to you, and tell the group why you found them meaningful.

3. Pray for one another, asking God to help you identify your fears and develop your own faith statements. Use your worries to trigger a prayer similar to the one offered at the end of the chapter.

CHAPTER 12: RELAX YOUR GRIP

1. Have you ever thought that you could somehow prevent a negative outcome by worrying? Please explain.

2. What ideas in this chapter did you find helpful, and why were they particularly meaningful at this time in your life?

3. Pray for one another, asking God to help each group member become proficient in using the techniques learned in this class. Ask God to lead you into peace, and make a commitment to take His hand and hang on for all you're worth.

Multnomah Publishers

The publisher and author would love to hear your comments about this book. *Please contact us at:*
www.multnomah.net/lettinggo

APPENDIX A

WHEN IS MEDICAL INTERVENTION HELPFUL?

ASSESSING THE NEED

Clinical research shows that one out of four people will suffer an anxiety disorder during his lifetime.[1] All people worry and feel anxious from time to time, but not everyone develops an anxiety disorder. When mental health professionals assess for an anxiety disorder, they look at the frequency, duration, and severity of specific symptoms and how much they are impairing a person's performance and quality of life.

CATEGORIES OF ANXIETY DISORDERS

There are several categories of anxiety disorders:

Generalized Anxiety Disorder (GAD)

A person suffering from GAD may say that he can't remember a time when he *didn't* feel anxious. His bodily sensations signal that danger is just around the corner, and he lives in a state of endless worry that an accident is going to happen at any moment. He is usually worried about two or more of the circumstances of his life and feels on edge, irritable, and in perpetual fight/flight mode. It's as if his body is wired at a higher voltage, which leads him to overreact to small stimuli. This sensitivity can be seen in early childhood and is attributed in part to an inherited predisposition. Difficult circumstances can trigger anxiety, but even after a problematic situation is resolved, a person with GAD is unable to turn off the worries in his mind or calm the physical excitation that anxiety produces.

120

Panic Disorder (PD)

A person with panic disorder lives with a sudden and intense fear of impending doom, which typically triggers symptoms such as a racing and pounding heart, sweating, trembling, shaking, shortness of breath, choking, chest pain, difficulty swallowing, nausea, dizziness, fear of losing control or going crazy, fear of dying, chills, numbness, or hot flashes. Feelings of panic usually peak within three to ten minutes from the onset of an attack and then subside. The interaction between the physical sensations and the person's fear of them is very strong. He dreads the next attack and may begin to avoid places where a panic attack has occurred. Panic disorder typically begins following a period of increased stress.

Phobia

A phobia is an intense dislike or fear of some situation or thing. The two most common phobias are *specific* phobia, a fear of a specific thing like flying, driving, heights, spiders, enclosed spaces, or crowds; and *social* phobia, a consistent anxiety about situations in which a person is exposed to possible scrutiny by others and fears that he may act in a way that will be humiliating or embarrassing. Social fears may be related to public speaking, meeting new people, or attending social functions. A person with a social phobia is so anxious about situations like these that his fear limits his activity and impairs his ability to function.

Obsessive-Compulsive Disorder (OCD)

Obsessions are unwanted thoughts and impulses that repeatedly surface in the mind, causing increased anxiety. Typical obsessions include having to have everything in perfect order, aggressive thoughts of hurting one's self or others, sexual images, concerns about contamination, and doubts about whether or not something was closed or turned off after leaving a location. Compulsive behaviors are the rituals people devise to relieve the anxiety produced by such intrusive thoughts. Common compulsions include perfectionistic cleaning and organizing, constant demands for reassurance, excessive hand-washing and showering, and disproportionate checking of doors, lights, and appliances. Although 80 percent of the population claim to experience obsessions now and then, a person suffering with OCD is unable to turn off obsessive thoughts even though he would like to. He usually knows that his impulses and actions are problematic but is unable to stop them on his own.

Post-Traumatic Stress Disorder (PTSD)

A person with PTSD has endured or witnessed a trauma so severe that it has left him with a heightened sense of anxiety and feelings of loss of control. Symptoms include flashbacks, reliving the event, nightmares, living on guard, and perpetually scanning the horizon for potential danger. If these symptoms appear a month or more after the trauma, the diagnosis is PTSD;

if they appear within the first month following the trauma, the diagnosis is Acute Stress Disorder (ASD).

WHEN TO TREAT WORRY AND ANXIETY SYMPTOMS WITH MEDICATION

The brain is like any other organ in the body. It can have imperfections and not function properly for one reason or another. But a wealth of research indicates that medical intervention coupled with cognitive behavioral therapy can bring tremendous relief to someone whose symptoms meet the diagnostic threshold of the categories mentioned above. Medications can balance the brain chemistry so that a person does not have to suffer from intense worry and anxiety for the rest of his life.

Did you know that there are more nerve cells in the brain than there are people on earth? Each nerve cell is like a small computer, capable of recognizing pattern, giving and receiving information, and networking with thousands of other small computers. Imagine every person on earth having one thousand arms and being able to reach out and connect them with all the other arms of every other person on earth. That gives a small picture of the complexity of the networking of the human brain.

Trauma and prolonged periods of stress can deplete the chemicals in the brain that are responsible for mood, concentration, focus, motivation, and overall peace of mind. Chemicals such as serotonin, noripenephrine, and dopamine transmit messages from one cell to the next in the brain; GABA (gamma amino butyric acid) inhibits excitement and modulates fear and other strong emotions. When these chemicals are depleted, message transmission is impaired, and a person may experience symptoms of anxiety and/or depression.

Some medications used to treat severe symptoms of worry and anxiety help the brain function the way it is meant to by correcting chemical imbalances. These medications can work in the brain like a cast or splint works on a broken arm: They can promote healing by supporting the nerve cells while a person learns the adaptive skills he needs to work with his anxieties. Some people, however, are reluctant to use medication because they fear that it will change their personality or that they will become addicted. A few "calming" medications of the older type could be addictive, but most of the medications approved for usage within the last two decades have no addictive properties. Fears about addiction or personality change are groundless, and they unnecessarily perpetuate suffering. When medications are applied appropriately (not one size fits all), they can help people recover from the symptoms of worry and anxiety.

With the right medication fit, side effects are minimal, and the individual doesn't notice anything different in the way he functions day to day. In a sense, the medication is like a good pair of glasses: It corrects his vision and enables him to see the world more clearly. It corrects the chemical imbalances in the brain that distorted his mental outlook in the first place. The better the medication fit, the less aware the individual is that the medication is doing anything other than helping him think straight and feel better.

Research shows that the majority of people who are treated with a combination of medication and cognitive behavioral therapy experience marked improvement and relief. On average, one-third of the individuals who use medication can discontinue the medicine within nine to twelve months; another third will need to use it intermittently through life; and the remaining third would benefit from ongoing use.

MEDICATIONS USED FOR ANXIETY DISORDERS

Medications commonly used to treat anxiety disorders fall under the following categories:

SSRIs: Selective Serotonin Re-uptake Inhibitors[2]

- Paxil, Zoloft, Luvox, Prozac, Celexa

Other Antidepressants[3]

- Tofranil: Effective for panic disorder; not effective for OCD, social phobia, or specific phobia.
- Anafrail: Effective for panic disorder and OCD; not effective for specific phobia.
- Effexor: Effective for GAD and panic disorder. More research needed.
- Serzone: Likely effective for panic disorder. More research needed.

Benzodiazepines

- Xanax, Klonapin, Valium, Ativan: Helpful for short-term, intermittent use to give quick relief for panic symptoms. When used long term and several times a day, they can be difficult to discontinue.
- Alprazolam and Clonazepam: Effective for panic disorder and social phobia.

- Diazepam and Lorazepam: Effective for GAD; not effective for specific phobia or OCD.

Serotonin Modulator

- Buspar: Effective for GAD, this medicine selectively blocks some of the serotonin sites that appear to cause anxiety.

Antiseizure Medications

- Gabitril: One of several medications for treating seizure disorders that are being used experimentally to reduce anxiety by increasing the brain's own GABA. (Gabitril blocks the reuptake of GABA in the brain.)

ANXIETY AND HORMONES

Many women experience heightened anxiety during days twenty-one through twenty-eight of their menstrual cycle. This is due largely to a drop in progesterone, a natural antianxiety hormone that peaks in a woman's body on the twenty-first day and then begins to decline. As it decreases, irritability, agitation, and anxiety can become more pronounced.

In contrast, increased levels of progesterone have a sedating, tiring impact and can trigger depression. One out of three teenagers has suffered clinical depression after receiving a shot of Depoprovera (long-acting birth control agent that is high in progesterone). If a man is given increased levels of progesterone, he may become suppressed, lethargic, unable to get out of bed, or apathetic.

Progesterone enhances monoamine oxidase (MAO), the enzyme that breaks down and gets rid of serotonin. Estrogen, on the other hand, inhibits the breakdown of MAO, thus enhancing the buildup of serotonin. On the fourteenth day of a woman's menstrual cycle, when progesterone is rising, the breakdown and loss of serotonin in the brain accelerates, which can lead to feelings of depression and anxiety later in the month.

Some physicians are now suggesting that an anti-depressant be taken on a couple of specified days between day fourteen and day twenty-one, when estrogen is on the decline and progesterone is on the rise. This "pulse dosing" boosts the serotonin levels in the brain, which in turn relieves agitation and anxiety later in the month (see diagram).[4]

HORMONAL FLUCTUATIONS IN 28-DAY CYCLE

used by permisson of Dr. Warner Swarner, M.D.

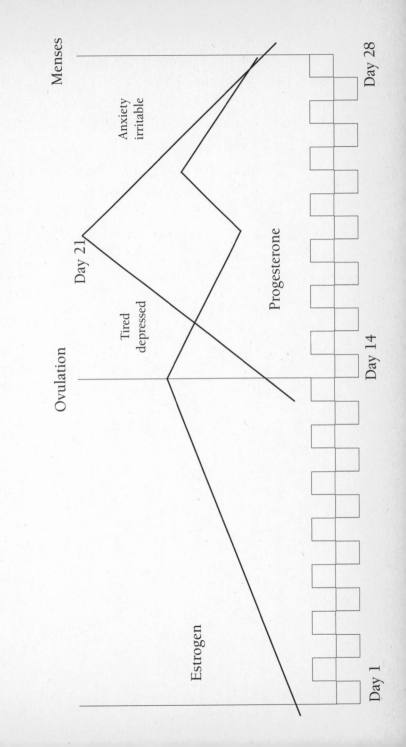

Menses

Anxiety
irritable

Day 21

Tired
depressed

Ovulation

Progesterone

Estrogen

Day 1

Day 14

Day 28

PPENDIX B

SCRIPTURES TO CALM
A WORRIED MIND

WORRIES ABOUT DEATH

Jesus said… "I am the resurrection and the life. He who believes in me will live, even though he dies; and whoever lives and believes in me will never die." —JOHN 11:25–26

Even though I walk through the valley of the shadow of death, I will fear no evil, for you are with me; your rod and your staff, they comfort me…. Surely goodness and love will follow me all the days of my life.—PSALM 23:4, 6

WORRIES ABOUT THE FUTURE

The unfailing love of the LORD never ends! By his mercies we have been kept from complete destruction. Great is his faithfulness; his mercies begin afresh each day. —LAMENTATIONS 3:22–23, NLT

I will send down showers in season; there will be showers of blessing. —EZEKIEL 34:26

The LORD is faithful to all his promises. —PSALM 145:13

Surely I am with you always. —MATTHEW 28:20

There is surely a future hope for you, and your hope will not be cut off. —PROVERBS 23:18

"For I know the plans I have for you," declares the LORD, "plans to prosper you and not to harm you, plans to give you hope and a future. Then you will call upon me and come and pray to me, and I will listen to you. You will seek me and find me when you seek me with all your heart. I will be found by you," declares the LORD. —JEREMIAH 29:11–14

WORRIES ABOUT PAST MISTAKES

"And we know that in all things God works for the good of those who love him." —ROMANS 8:28

My God turns my darkness into light. —PSALM 18:28

If we confess our sins, he is faithful and just and will forgive us our sins and purify us from all unrighteousness. —1 JOHN 1:9

Confess your sins to each other and pray for each other so that you may be healed. —JAMES 5:16

WORRIES ABOUT MANAGING OUR PROBLEMS

"My grace is sufficient for you, for my power is made perfect in weakness." —2 CORINTHIANS 12:9

Jesus told his disciples…that they should always pray and not give up. —LUKE 18:1

And my God will meet all your needs. —Philippians 4:19

When I called, you answered me; you made me bold and stout-hearted.—Psalm 138:3

We went through fire and water, but you brought us to a place of abundance.—Psalm 66:12

They were at their wits' end. Then they cried out to the Lord in their trouble, and he brought them out of their distress.
—Psalm 107:27–28

He knows the way that I take; when he has tested me, I will come forth as gold.—Job 23:10

Worries about Our Children

Know therefore that the Lord your God is God; he is the faithful God, keeping his covenant of love to a thousand generations of those who love him and keep his commands.
—Deuteronomy 7:9

"'In the last days, God says, I will pour out my Spirit on all people. Your sons and daughters will prophesy, your young men will see visions, your old men will dream dreams…. And everyone who calls on the name of the Lord will be saved.'"—Acts 2:17, 21

"I am the Lord, the God of all mankind. Is anything too hard for me?" —Jeremiah 32:27

I would have despaired unless I had believed that I would see the goodness of the Lord.... Wait for the Lord; be strong and let your heart take courage.—Psalm 27:13–14, nasb

"Everything is possible for him who believes."—Mark 9:23

Worries about Our Inadequacies

Not that we are competent in ourselves to claim anything for ourselves, but our competence comes from God.—2 Corinthians 3:5

I can do everything through him who gives me strength.

—Philippians 4:13

And God is able to make all grace abound to you, so that in all things at all times, having all that you need, you will abound in every good work.—2 Corinthians 9:8

"Let not the wise man boast of his wisdom or the strong man boast of his strength or the rich man boast of his riches, but let him who boasts boast about this: that he understands and knows me, that I am the Lord, who exercises kindness, justice and righteousness on earth, for in these I delight," declares the Lord.—Jeremiah 9:23–24

We were under great pressure...so that we despaired even of life.... But this happened that we might not rely on ourselves but on God, who raises the dead.—2 Corinthians 1:8–9

"The eyes of the Lord range throughout the earth to strengthen those whose hearts are fully committed to him."—2 Chronicles 16:9

WORRIES ABOUT OUR VALUE AND WORTH

You are precious and honored in my sight, and…I love you.
—ISAIAH 43:4

Whoever touches you touches the apple of his eye.—ZECHARIAH 2:8

How precious are your thoughts about me, O God! They are innumerable! I can't even count them; they outnumber the grains of sand! And when I wake up in the morning, you are still with me!—PSALM 139:17–18, NLT

He delights in me.—PSALM 18:19, NLT

"I have loved you with an everlasting love."—JEREMIAH 31:3

WORRIES ABOUT FAILURE

In all these things we are more than conquerors through him who loved us. For I am convinced that neither death nor life, neither angels nor demons, neither the present nor the future, nor any powers, neither height nor depth, nor anything else in all creation, will be able to separate us from the love of God that is in Christ Jesus our Lord.—ROMANS 8:37–39

But remember the LORD your God, for it is he who gives you the ability… —DEUTERONOMY 8:18

"With everlasting kindness I will have compassion on you," says the LORD your Redeemer.—ISAIAH 54:8

The LORD upholds all those who fall and lifts up all who are bowed down.—PSALM 145:14

WORRIES ABOUT HARM AND DANGER

"The LORD your God is with you, he is mighty to save. He will take great delight in you, he will quiet you with his love, he will rejoice over you with singing." —ZEPHANIAH 3:17

"'Not by might nor by power, but by my Spirit,' says the LORD Almighty." —ZECHARIAH 4:6

"This is what the LORD says to you: 'Do not be afraid or discouraged because of this vast army. For the battle is not yours, but God's.'" —2 CHRONICLES 20:15

For he will command his angels concerning you to guard you in all your ways. —PSALM 91:11

Though I walk in the midst of trouble, you preserve my life. —PSALM 138:7

WORRIES ABOUT DECISIONS

If any of you lacks wisdom, he should ask God, who gives generously to all without finding fault, and it will be given to him. —JAMES 1:5

Your hand will guide me, your right hand will hold me fast. —PSALM 139:10

"[He will] guide our feet into the path of peace." —LUKE 1:79

Whether you turn to the right or to the left, your ears will hear a voice behind you, saying, "This is the way; walk in it." —ISAIAH 30:21

The LORD will guide you always; he will satisfy your needs.
—ISAIAH 58:11

For this God is our God for ever and ever; he will be our guide even to the end.—PSALM 48:14

"We do not know what to do, but our eyes are upon you."
—2 CHRONICLES 20:12

WORRIES ABOUT THE TIMING OF SOMETHING IMPORTANT

My times are in your hands.—PSALM 31:15

Now is the time of God's favor.—2 CORINTHIANS 6:2

"Be still, and know that I am God." —PSALM 46:10

"You do not realize now what I am doing, but later you will understand."—JOHN 13:7

GENERAL WORRIES

Let us therefore make every effort to do what leads to peace.
—ROMANS 14:19

Take courage…take courage…. Take courage and work, for I am with you, says the LORD Almighty. My Spirit remains among you, just as I promised…. So do not be afraid.—HAGGAI 2:4–5, NLT

Do not be anxious about anything, but in everything, by prayer and petition, with thanksgiving, present your requests to God. And the peace of God, which transcends all understanding, will guard your hearts and your minds in Christ Jesus.
—PHILIPPIANS 4:6–7

Do not fret.—PSALM 37:1

"According to your faith will it be done to you." —MATTHEW 9:29

"Until now you have not asked for anything in my name. Ask and you will receive, and your joy will be complete."—JOHN 16:24

"Test me in this…and see if I will not throw open the floodgates of heaven and pour out so much blessing that you will not have room enough for it."—MALACHI 3:10

Without faith it is impossible to please God, because anyone who comes to him must believe that he exists and that he rewards those who earnestly seek Him.—HEBREWS 11:6

[Jesus said,] "My peace I give you."—JOHN 14:27

We give great honor to those who endure under suffering. Job is an example of a man who endured patiently. From his experience we see how the Lord's plan finally ended in good, for he is full of tenderness and mercy.—JAMES 5:11, NLT

We live by faith, not by sight.—2 CORINTHIANS 5:7

Let him who walks in the dark, who has no light, trust in the name of the LORD and rely on his God.—ISAIAH 50:10

The LORD longs to be gracious to you; he rises to show you compassion.—ISAIAH 30:18

"I am coming soon. Hold on to what you have, so that no one will take your crown." —REVELATION 3:11

$\mathcal{N}$OTES

INTRODUCTION

1. Adapted from Pam Vredevelt, *Angel Behind the Rocking Chair* (Sisters, Ore.: Multnomah Publishers, 1997), 21–3.
2. Anne G. Perkins, "Medical Costs," *Harvard Business Review* 72, no. 6 (November/December 1994): 12.
3. Frank Minerth, Paul Meier, Don Hawkins, *Worry-Free Living* (Nashville, Tenn.: Thomas Nelson Publishers, 1989), 17.
4. Martin Anthony, "Understanding Anxiety: Effects on Mental and Physical Health," symposium at Oregon Convention Center, 24 May 2001, Portland, Oregon.
5. If you have difficulty using these strategies, or find that your uneasy state of mind persists while using them, you might want to consider consulting a professional therapist. Trained, objective guides can help teach you how to let go of worry and anxiety.

CHAPTER 2

1. Adapted from Pam Vredevelt, *Espresso for a Woman's Spirit* (Sisters, Ore.: Multnomah Publishers, 2000), 22–6.
2. Ibid., 27–8.

CHAPTER 6

1. Adapted from Pam Vredevelt, *Letting Go of Disappointments and Painful Losses* (Multnomah Publishers, Inc.), 91–2.
2. Ibid., 88.

CHAPTER 7

1. Dr. Mike Ladra, "Conquering Fear," adapted from a message given by the senior pastor at First Presbyterian Church, Salinas, California, 1999.

CHAPTER 8

1. Robert Krant and Vicky Lundmark, "Internet Paradox: A Social Technology That Reduces Social Involvement and Psychological Well-Being?" *American Psychologist* 53, no. 9 (September 1998): 1017–31.

CHAPTER 9

1. Adapted from Pam Vredevelt, *Espresso for a Woman's Spirit, Book 2* (Sisters, Ore.: Multnomah Publishers, 2001), 23–7.

CHAPTER II

1. Brennan Manning, *Ruthless Trust: The Ragamuffin's Path to God* (San Francisco: HarperSanFrancisco, 2000), 96.
2. Matthew Henry's Commentary on Matthew 8:5–13 in *The PC Study Bible Complete Reference Library* (Seattle: Biblesoft, 1992), 24.
3. Manning, *Ruthless Trust,* 11–2.
4. Adapted from Pam Vredevelt, *Espresso for a Woman's Spirit* (Sisters, Ore.: Multnomah Publishers, 2000), 35–43.

Chapter 12

1. Pam Vredevelt, *Letting Go of Disappointments and Painful Losses* (Sisters, Ore.: Multnomah Publishers, 2001), 16–7.

Appendix A

1. For ease of reading, the masculine pronoun is used to refer to both males and females.
2. These medicines effectively reduce anxiety symptoms for all above categories except specific phobia.
3. Beta blockers such as Atenolol and Propanolol are not effective for treating anxiety disorders but may reduce physical symptoms such as trembling.
4. The information in the section regarding medications used to treat anxiety was taken from an interview with Dr. Warner Swarner, M.D., a psychiatrist who specializes in treating anxiety and depression and an internationally known clinical educator in the field.

How to Say Good-bye to Pain

Professional counselor Pam Vredevelt constantly hears the question, "How do I let go of the pain I feel?" Whether it is a soured friendship or an unsatisfying job, a wayward child, or unrealistic expectations, every person has to deal with lingering disappointment and its clouding effect on attitude and relationships. God does not intend that pain to cripple, distort, and consume his children. Getting "unstuck" is possible, Pam writes, through the use of a few simple and practical tools that lead to peace of mind and tranquility of heart. We've all heard the expression, "Let go and let God." With compassion and warmth, Pam Vredevelt shows how.

ISBN 1-57673-954-6

Enjoy Spiritual Energy throughout the Day with Stories from *Pam Vredevelt*

Espresso for Your Spirit

In engaging, humorous, and often poignant vignettes, bestselling author Pam Vredevelt serves up cup after cup of energizing espresso to encourage the spirits of overwhelmed and exhausted parents.

ISBN 1-57673-485-4

Espresso for a Woman's Spirit

Exhaustion doesn't have to be habit-forming! Overcome it with humorous and poignant vignettes that bring refreshment to the soul the way espresso brings energy to the body.

ISBN 1-57673-636-9

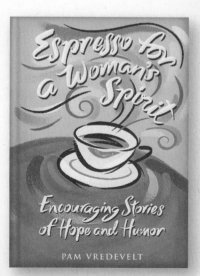

A Fresh Java Jolt for the Weary

No one has limitless resources. Sooner or later, every one of us will find our cup of enthusiasm draining or even downright dry. But just as espresso jump-starts a sluggish mind, *Espresso for a Woman's Spirit, Book 2* will reenergize the lagging spirit! Pam Vredevelt's funny and poignant real-life stories remind readers that God is always faithful, always at work, and always full of everything we lack, including guidance, love, compassion, and strength. Each "sip" of this heart-warming book provides just the right amount of get-up-and-go for those whose vigor has "gotten up and gone."

ISBN 1-57673-986-4

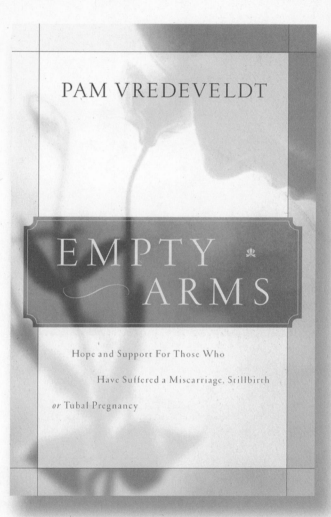

PAM VREDEVELDT

EMPTY ❀
ARMS

Hope and Support For Those Who

Have Suffered a Miscarriage, Stillbirth

or Tubal Pregnancy

Having lost a child, the author writes with compassionate insight to women and their families, addressing grief, anger, guilt, spiritual battles, and other pertinent topics.

ISBN 1-57673-851-5

In Your Darkest Place, You May Find a Glimpse of Glory

Angel

Behind

the
Rocking

Stories of Hope in Unexpected Places

Chair

Pam Vredevelt

Brimming with moving personal stories, *Angel Behind the Rocking Chair* offers hope and encouragement to those facing unexpected adversity. Each story is a reassuring reminder of God's unfailing love.

ISBN 1-57673-644-X